Coleman Grocery a₁

In the 50's-60's- and 70's a little country store located just north of the Telfair County line, in Dodge County, sandwiched between US 341 Highway and the Southern Railroad was once the Mecca for locals and weary travelers alike. The Colemans, William Henry and Hazel, not only operated the store, but several days a week Mr. Coleman loaded up his old step van, he called the rolling store, with canned goods, flour, sugar, fresh meats, fish, and milk and traveled the countryside delivering groceries with a hand-shake and a smile.

Mr. William Henry, as I called him, filled the customers' orders left under a rock on the porch or in an empty jar on a fence post by the gate. Many times the customers would be out working in the fields and Mr. Coleman would put the perishable items in the refrigerator and the groceries in the cabinets. Nobody locked their houses back then, so he entered home after home on his Monday-Thursday routes.

Mrs. Hazel, a small woman with a big heart and a big smile would have to operate the store by herself on those days. She pumped gas, ran the register, on top of cooking, cleaning, and raising four children. For many years the only running water supplied to the store was a single faucet just outside the back door. Mrs. Hazel had to fill pans with water and tote them inside and set them on a table to wash clothes, dishes, and themselves. When a simple hole was drilled through the back wall of the store, just above the lone faucet and an extra one was installed inside the

building. Mrs. Hazel cried tears of joy. With all the
modern conveniences we have today and are pretty well
taken for granted, I still remember how tears of joy poured
from her eyes over a simple faucet. This hard working
family never complained as they put in 12-14 hour days
365 times a year. As darkness fell on the little country
store surrounded by tall pine trees, the multi-colored neon
lights that ran along the eves of the building would let
people know that they were still open.

You could set your watch by the store's daily regulars.
Mr. Teal dropped off the dry-cleaned clothes at 10:00 a.m.
for the many families who lived on the dirt roads that criss-
crossed the area like a jigsaw puzzle. At 12:00 noon you
could hear Mr. Watson blow the whistle signaling lunch
time from the turpentine plant in Helena. At 1:00 p.m. a
white Ford car drove by the front door and delivered the
Macon newspaper. The Milan brothers arrived at 2:00 p.
m. on their 8-N Ford tractors to have a cold soft drink and
catch up on the local news. At 2:30 Vernon Young came
by to deliver fresh bread. At 3:00 p.m. when the big
shining brown passenger train came by going north, the
Milan brothers knew it was time to go back to farming.
Mr. Tom Whatley would arrive at 3:30 p.m. and if I was
lucky enough to be there when he arrived, he would buy me
a soft drink and a cookie from the cookie barrel that sat on
the check-out counter. Mr. Parker would arrive around
4:00 p.m. on the way from his job in town for a bottle of
cola before going to work on his farm.

The constant arrival and departure of people reminded
me of ants moving to and fro from an ant hill. Many

people up north would travel this route on the way to Jacksonville and Daytona Beach, Florida. The Coleman's would remember them by name and welcome them with a smile.

As the years rolled by, the Coleman's sons, Doyle and Waymon, both married local girls and left home to start stores of their own, following in their parents' footsteps. As the Coleman's two daughters grew into pretty young ladies, I realized they had both inherited their mother's special smile and like their parents, they never met a stranger.

As the sixties turned into the seventies, Mr. William Henry Coleman died of a heart attack. Mrs. Hazel closed the little store and moved to town to raise her daughters. The lonely little store sat by the side of the road and collected cobwebs. The paint peeled and the shingles cracked! Years later, in the name of progress, US 341 was four-laned and became the Golden Isles Parkway. The weathered little store that had been a center of excitement and constant activity was no more.

As the sands of time flow through the hourglass of our lives, we need to keep the memories of a peaceful time stored in our hearts, because places like the Coleman's Grocery and Rolling Store only happen once, but memories can last forever.

Fireman Story

When the sands of time flow through the hourglass of our lives, some memories stick to our hearts. One of those memories goes back in time to when I was about five years old. I had come down with a fever and my throat was sore. My parents knew I needed to see a doctor. I wasn't really happy about that, because I was afraid I would get a shot. My threshold of pain has always been very low, but I was five and whatever my parents said would be what happened.

My parents drove me to our favorite doctor's office, but he had a sign on the door, "Sorry, Closed until Monday."

My Dad and I were both disappointed, but we drove on to the medical clinic up the street. It was a long red brick building surrounded by large oak trees and had shrubbery about three feet high all the way around the building.

When my name was called, my parents walked me down the hall led by one of the doctor's secretaries to room number six. In just a few minutes, but it felt like hours, one of the doctors come into the room wearing a white shirt and had a stethoscope hanging around his neck.

"What's wrong, little fellow?" He asked.

Mother answered, "He has a fever and says his throat is hurting."

He picked me up and set me on his examining table, told me to open wide, and crammed a piece of wood about the size of a 2 x 4 down my throat and said, "Say Ahh."

Now why do they always say that? Why not say your name or count to ten or recite the Gettysburg Address, but no, it's always say Ahh.

I screeched out as close as I could the Ahh the doctor requested. Before I had finished, he said, "Strep Throat. A big shot of penicillin will cure that, along with bed rest and plenty of fluids."

The part that stuck-out in my mind was B-I-G shot of penicillin. The fact that I was going to have to suffer the horrible pain of having a needle stuck in my butt was bad enough, but he said, "B-I-G shot of penicillin.

I was scared to death, so when Dad remarked that the new fire department station is finally complete next door and he and Mom stretched to look out the window to see the structure across the street and while the doctor was busy filling a needle about the size of a fence post with a milky white looking stuff, I slipped off the examining table and ran out the door.

I raced down the hall to the back door and then outside. The only place I could see to hide was behind the shrubbery that circled the building, so I ran around the corner to the front side away from the end door of the building and hid behind one of the bushes.

It wasn't long before I heard my Mom and Dad calling my name, but I stayed put. All I could think about was the word BIG and shot.

In a few minutes a man in a nice uniform comes walking across the street from the new fire department building. I figured he must have been the fire chief, because of his fancy uniform. The fireman stopped right beside the bush I was hiding behind and just turned and looked away.

"Are you the one they're hunting for?" he asked me without even looking at me.

"Yes, I guess I am." I whispered.

"Why are you hiding, kid?" the man asked in a very gentle voice.

"The doctor was going to give me a really big shot." I whispered.

"Why was he going to do that?" the fireman asked, still looking away.

"I'm sick. I've got a sore throat and a fever." I whispered.

I could still hear my parents as they called my name again and again. I don't think they knew whether I was outside the doctor's clinic or inside, but other people were now joining the hunt.

"Do you think the doctor was going to give you that shot just to hurt you or was he trying to help you?" the fireman asked again without looking.

"I guess he wanted to help me get well." I whispered.

"Young fellow, sometimes we have to experience a little pain in order to appreciate feeling good." The fireman said.

"I know, but that needle was huge." I whispered.

"You know, if you were a big boy, I would take you across the street and let you sit in our new fire truck and ring the bell," The fireman said.

"I'm a big boy," I responded.

"A big boy would be big enough to take the doctor's shot, so he could get well," Said the fireman.

"I guess I shouldn't have run away, should I?" I said.

"You know, son, it's a normal reaction for all of us to try to run away from problems," he said.

"I guess I did wrong, didn't I, Sir?" I said.

"Well, it's not too late before your parents start panicking. Let's go back inside," said the fireman.

Now I was scared of the shot. "My parents are probably mad and will spank me," I said.

"What if I walk you back inside and explain to your parents that you were just a little nervous and decided to go for a walk first. You can get your shot, and then we'll walk across the street together, so you can sit in my new fire truck and ring the bell," the fireman said.

"OK," I said, as I walked around behind the bush.

The fireman reached out his hand and talked to me about what a big boy I was and he opened the door to the doctor's clinic.

My parents were very relieved to see me and my new friend and I took my shot like a big boy.

Then the fireman, my parents, and I crossed the street, so that I could sit in the new fire truck and ring the bell. This fine man had helped me through a bad situation. The needle was the only pain my bottom felt that day.

A few years before this incident, a propane gas tank exploded in the adjoining small town of Helena and this very fireman and that very fire truck responded to the horrible blast that killed and injured so many. He bravely fought the blaze even after he himself was injured to try to save as many victims as possible.

The Governor proclaimed this brave fireman a hero. I didn't need the paper or the Governor to tell me that. I had figured that out by myself.

A Train Ride

I lived on a farm on the south side of D.C. That stands for Dodge County in Georgia. Our farm was about five miles from town and we didn't have any neighbors that had kids. I was shocked on my first day at school when I looked around the room at approximately 30 kinds about my size. I didn't think there were that many children in the whole world. I still remember the shock of being in the room with all of them. I guess I was like an only child, because my brothers were grown and my sister avoided me like the plague.

Our teacher, Mrs. Cadwell, a very sweet lady, introduced herself and had each one of us stand and introduce ourselves. When they got to me, I was so amazed I almost forgot my name. The kids all laughed and smiled. I think they thought I was just clowning around.

A few weeks later, my parents and I went to visit my aunt, uncle and cousins in Helena. My uncle worked for the railroad and I was always fascinated by his stories about trains. I would get my Mom or Dad to walk with me across the road from our home to watch the afternoon passenger train pass by. I loved to smile and wave at the passengers and the train's engineer and conductor. Now I realize that those people must have waved at me and thought, what a dumb kid!

My uncle was explaining to us that the last passenger train would run on Wednesday and the service would be discontinued. My heart was broken. Many times I had hoped and dreamed that someday I could go for a ride on that passenger train. My sister had ridden the train many times with my aunt and her daughter to shop in Macon, but I never got to go

My uncle must have noticed how disappointed I was and he asked me what was wrong. I looked down at the floor and told him I had always wanted to ride on that big, shiny passenger train and now I knew it would never happen. My uncle Luther was one of those people that could pull a surprise out of thin air, if you gave him a chance. I asked him, if there was any chance I might still get to ride the train someday.

He just patted me on my head and said, "Maybe someday."

I was so sad, but I knew life had to go on. The next Wednesday when I got to school, Mrs. Cadwell told us she had a wonderful surprise and that a very special person in our class had arranged for all of the first grade students to board a school bus and ride to Helena and then board the last passenger train to come through middle Georgia and return to Chauncey.

I thought to myself who this wonderful person could be who arranged for us to ride the train. It seemed like forever, but shortly after we returned from lunch, a big yellow bus pulled up and parked in front of our class. I couldn't wait any longer. I stood up and asked Mrs. Cadwell who the special person was that arranged for us to ride the train. All of the kids wanted to know who this person was.

Mrs. Cadwell said, "I will tell you when we get on the bus."

In a few minutes the principal knocked on the door and told us to line up and follow our teacher to the bus. I thought I am going to be best friends with this special person who got us a train ride for life, even if it was a girl!

We marched to the big yellow school bus, went up the stairs and found a seat. Then, I asked our teacher again who the special person was?

Mrs. Cadwell smiled and said, "It's you!"

Then she walked over to me and placed her hand on my head. The teacher said, "Children, you can thank this young man. He was disappointed when his uncle told him the passenger train's final trip through this part of the country would be today. His uncle called the head of the railroad and arranged for us to ride on the last train!"

I couldn't believe it. The other kids were yelling and cheering and smiling at me and saying, "Thank you."

I was raised in the country with no other kids around and I had felt so lonely. Even when I started to school, I noticed no one spoke to me, yet many of the other kids seemed to know each other. I was just a simple country boy. The other kids had pet dogs or cats. I had a pet cow named Ole Strawberry.

The ten mile bus ride to Helena took forever. I just couldn't wait. I had dreamed so many times about going on a train ride and I was afraid something might go wrong. I began to wonder was this real or was I going to wake up and realize that it's just another dream.

When we arrived at the Depot and exited the bus, I saw my uncle Luther standing out front of the big red and green building. I ran over to him and grabbed his leg and said, "Thank you so much!"

He reached down and picked me up and said, "You are welcome, big boy!

He put me down and showed all the kids how the Depot worked and explained that the train's horn was used like a Morse code system to communicate with the Depot and the conductor. He explained to us to stay inside the Depot building until the big shiny brown passenger train came to a complete stop and then wait for the conductor to lead us to the train.

Suddenly, I heard the whistle of the passenger train coming from the South. I just couldn't wait to get on board. I had dreamed of doing this so many times.

When the big train came to a stop, the conductor opened the door and then folded down some steps. The conductor's uniform made him look very important, but his smile showed that he liked kids. He stood to one side and motioned "this way" with his hand and said, "This way, young ladies and gentlemen."

I marched up the steps and was amazed at how nice the interior was. The big brown seats looked like they were made for royalty, instead of kids.

As we entered the large passenger car, my teacher explained to the well-dressed passengers that we would only be traveling to the next stop.

The seats were mostly empty and the passengers were seated along the sides next to the windows. The passengers stood up and gave the kids the window seats so we could enjoy the trip even more. The conductor once again told the passengers that the first graders would only be traveling to the next stop. I guess he wanted to assure the passengers that the noise and confusion would be over shortly.

The passengers were mostly older people, apparently on their way back from vacations in Florida. They were well-dressed and very kind and friendly. The conductor walked down the center of the passenger car with a big smile showing a gold tooth and said, "What a beautiful bunch of kids!"

One of the passengers, a well-dressed lady with gray hair, asked our teacher why we were riding the train.

My teacher placed her hand on my head and said, "Because this little kid with the brown hair was so sad when he heard this would be the last passenger train to come through here, his uncle, the Depot master, arranged this trip for all of them."

All of the passengers stood up and cheered and clapped their hands.

I was thinking that surely this isn't happening. I'm just dreaming.

The conductor yelled, "All aboard!" To be sure everybody was on the train.

As he stood in the doorway, he waved at the engineer and then it happened.

I could hear the roar of the big diesel engine as the train slowly moved forward. The big steel wheels made a creaking sound under our feet and the big train started moving and picking up speed.

Then it occurred to me, I might accidentally be able to see my house from the train's big window. I was sitting on the west side of the train, but our house was across US Highway 341 and a row of pine trees was between the train tracks and our home. I wished I could have told my Mom and Dad that I would be coming by in a few minutes as a passenger on the train instead of a dumb kid waving at the people from the big red clay banks along the side of the tracks.

It was hard to tell where we were. I had never seen the world from the railroad before. The train rumbled on, moving faster and faster. The horn blew time and again. I tried to remember the Morse code like signals my uncle had explained to me, but I was just too excited. I just hoped I could see my house; I was going to look really hard.

14

I knew the train ran right along beside the highway until it got about a mile from our house. Then the highway curved away from the railroad, but ran back together just above where we lived. The train rocked gently from side to side as it proceeded on toward our home.

I thought about all of the times I got my parents to walk with me across the highway to see the train. I could hardly believe this was happening. The big train moved on past the Whatley scuppernong sales stand, and then up ahead, I saw Pridgen's Truck Stop.

I looked around the train to see the smiling faces of the other children. They were really enjoying the ride. I noticed the other passengers; they were enjoying our excitement! They had the biggest smiles of all.

The conductor came down the aisle and passed out candy lollipops to the children and said, "Please don't open these on the train. Wait until you get home."

The little girl across from me yelled, "I'm going to save mine for my little brother."

The conductor stopped and handed her another lollipop and smiled and walked on.

I knew we were getting closer to our home and I tried to imagine what I would see from the train. I was so afraid I wouldn't be able to see our house, because of all the trees between the railroad tracks and the highway. I remembered Dad had a big white storage building just before I would get to see our house, if I could manage to see it, then maybe, just maybe I could see our house.

The Coleman family had a country store just past our house on the land between the railroad and the highway. I could see it, even if I couldn't see our house. Just past the store was a dirt road that led to the larger part of our farm on the west side of the railroad tracks. The train's horn blew several times. I knew we were approaching the dirt road just past the Coleman's country store.

Suddenly, there it was! Dad's big white storage building and I could see our house through all the pine trees. I could still see our big white house with black shutters beside the windows.

The train continued on and I saw the big clay banks where I had stood so many times and waved at the passengers on the train. The next thing I saw was the back of the Coleman's family store. The Coleman's were a wonderful family and we were very fortunate to have these fine people for neighbors.

Then suddenly, I couldn't believe my eyes! I saw my Mom and Dad standing in front of our car parked on the little dirt road just past the Coleman's store. They were smiling and waving and I jumped to my feet screaming, "That's my Mom and Dad! That's my Mom and Dad!" at the top of my lungs!

The train lumbered on past two ponds between the railroad tracks and highway and then on past the Jaybird Springs dirt road. I was so excited! Everything looked different from the railroad as I tried to soak up a lifetime of memories from one train ride.

I suddenly realized I was standing in the nice brown seat. As I looked around, everybody was staring at me, but every face had a smile! I apologized to the older man next to me for yelling so loud.

He just smiled and said, "I love to see someone so excited, you can yell all you want to!"

I then glanced across the passenger car to see my teacher, Mrs. Cadwell.

Fortunately, she was smiling and winked at me and whispered, "It's alright."

I will never forget this kind sweet lady. I sat back down and watched carefully as our little white country church came into view, then past Zion Hope Church and Silver Haden Truck Stop. I realized this ride would end soon, but I wished it could go on forever.

The train's gentle vibration and pleasant rumble of the steel wheels gave a soothing effect. I could see why people smiled while traveling by rail. The train rumbled past the Jaybird Springs paved road and I could see the cows in the pastures to the west, just across the highway. The engineer continued to blow the horn as we came to several crossings along the way. The view from the large windows was like a movie of people, places, and things constantly changing.

As the train passed several homes, I realized the images would be forever printed in my brain. Like a tape recorder,

I would play them back again and again. We rounded a curve and I could tell the train was slowing down as we approached the small town of Chauncey.

The train slowed as we saw our school across the highway to our west and our country's flag flapping proudly in the breeze on a pole near the circular driveway. We rolled past several big white houses and then as the train slowed to a crawl, I saw Moore's Candy Company, just before the train came to a stop at the Chauncey Depot.

I wished I was Jesse James so I could commandeer the big shiny passenger train and keep going, but I knew that the trip was over. I just couldn't believe what had just taken place. A ride on the space shuttle wouldn't take the place of a simple ten mile train ride with my first grade classmates. I wonder how many of them remember this little piece of their past. I hope they do.

As I think of it now, if I had just dropped dead right there, it would have been the perfect ending for a little ugly freckle-faced boy raised alone out in the country. A kid who was so lonely, he had to have imaginary friends to play with. A kid who felt so insignificant and unimportant to this world to have such a beautiful event take place was more than my simple little mind could comprehend.

Great men from history conquered large parts of the world and probably didn't feel the satisfaction I got from a simple train ride. It's been over fifty years since that very special fall day in September, but I have kept this story stored in a special place in my heart and every time I hear a train blow its horn, for just a split second, I think about what a wonderful gift my Uncle Luther gave me and sixty other little kids, a gift I will treasure forever.

The Strawberry Cow

In the fall of 1960, I lived on a farm, just north of McRae, Georgia, on US Highway 341. It was one of those hot muggy afternoons, but a gentle rain had cooled things down while we ate supper. Afterwards, I decided to walk to the far corner of our property to a swing that hung from a large limb of an even larger oak tree. I had decided to swing for a while to cool off. My Father had decided to take a nap on the sofa and Mom was busy singing as she washed the dishes. I had just started swinging and was trying to reach the leaves that were on the outer branches of the tree when I heard a terrible loud series of KA-Boom, KA-Boom, and KA-Boom!

The noises came from across the highway and behind the small country store that sat between US 341 and the Southern Railroad. I quickly brought my swing to a sudden halt, as I saw a black Ford pickup coming across the railroad on a dirt road that circled around behind the northern portion of our farm and came out on US 341, just a few hundred feet north of the store. The black pickup's engine roared as the two occupants proceeded north on the highway. The tires made a screeching sound as they made contact with the pavement. I was frightened by the extremely loud noises and ran to our house. The afternoon haze had held the noise to the ground and had intensified the horror of the loud noises.

Mom met me at the door and asked, "What in the world was that terrible noise?"

I was a little short of breath after the race to our house, but I managed to say, "I don't know, but it was so loud, it scared me!"

The loud noises even woke my Father up. Neither thunder, nor lightning could do that. My Father stood up with a shocked look on his face and asked, "What in the world was that?"

My Mom responded, "I don't know. Was it thunder or some kind of explosion?"

My Father yawned and then asked, "Where did it come from?"

I said, "They came from over behind the store, somewhere across the railroad tracks."

My Dad asked, "How do you know?"

I said, "I was swinging in my swing under the big oak tree when I heard those terrible loud noises, then I saw a black pickup truck coming across the railroad tracks on the dirt road and race away up the highway, squealing its tires."

My Dad's facial expressions changed as he said, "That's it. The pickup's engine must have been back-firing; there's nothing to worry about."

The suspense about the loud noises came to a screeching halt when my Mom reminded us that it was nearly time for my favorite television show, Bonanza. We turned the television on, and relaxed and watched the show. The events of the evening drifted away in our minds.

The next morning Mom had a beautiful breakfast on the table, as usual. We ate breakfast and then got dressed for church. My Father was still a little curious about the noises from the night before and decided to make a quick trip across the highway and railroad to circle around our farm and check the cows. We had about a dozen cows, because we sold timber and turpentine. The cows were beneficial in that they ate the underbrush so that the trees didn't have to compete for the sun and rain. Also, the cows' hooves broke the crust of the soil so that rain could soak down into the soil, and of course, they fertilized the trees as well. We had some black cows, red cows, and some black and white cows, but my favorite was a white cow with red spots, we called 'Ole Strawberry'. This cow was so tame my Dad would just pick me up and set me on her back and walk along with her while she took me for a ride. This cow was so tame and gentle that we made it a pet and Dad had a leather belt engraved with 'Ole Strawberry' on it to hold a small brass bell around her neck. This is how we could check on the cows.

My Dad would blow the horn in our car and then we could get out and listen for the bell. The other cows would follow 'Ole Strawberry' as she came to the sound of the car's horn. We stopped on the road in front of the farm and Dad blew the horn several times and then shut the engine off to listen for the bell. He waited a few minutes and then he blew the horn again. I could tell Dad was concerned by the expression on his face.

Dad blew the horn again and finally we heard noises coming from the wooded area beyond the open pasture, then we saw the cows as they entered the pasture. Then my Dad said, "Oh no, hold on!" as he drove away.

I asked my Dad, "Where's 'Ole Strawberry'?"

My Father didn't answer as he drove quickly down the dirt road and pointed up ahead at something, as he stopped and drove over the stop gap. Now, a stop gap was an open pit with a heavy framed wooden board mesh built over it. You could drive across it, but livestock wouldn't cross over it. It was much better than opening a gate. I looked up to see what he was pointing to. It was a bunch of buzzards circling around just ahead of us. My Father brought our car to a sudden stop, opened the door, jumped out, and ran toward something just ahead of our car. As usual, I followed my Dad. Then, my Dad stopped and dropped to his knees, as my eyes focused on what he had seen. Ole Strawberry lay dead on the ground in front of us. My heart sank as I gazed at a cow that had been so tame and gentle. It would follow you around the farm as you worked.

My Father pointed to the cow's head and shouted, "Three gunshot wounds, somebody shot her!"

I asked my Dad, "Why would anybody shoot Ole Strawberry?"

My Father responded, "I don't know, I guess mean people do mean things!"

My stomach felt weak as I fought back the tears over Ole Strawberry, because little boys aren't supposed to cry!

My Father looked up and shouted, "Those loud noises must have been gunshots!"

I just kept asking myself, "How could anyone be so cruel!"

Then Dad shouted, "The bell is missing!"

My Dad stood up and looked around. He saw something and walked over and picked up a brown bottle. He held it with two fingers like it was the filthiest thing on earth and said, "It's a liquor bottle!"

Then Dad pointed to some tire tracks and said those tire tracks led back to the stop gap. Then he pointed again and said, "See those foot prints. There were two of them and they were wearing boots."

As my Dad walked around looking for evidence I knelt down and patted 'Ole Strawberry' on her back and whispered, "I'm sorry, I'm so sorry!"

My Father walked to our car and returned with a writing pad. He started writing on the pad as he walked around, then he stopped and started drawing something.

I asked, "What are you drawing?"

My Dad said, "I'm drawing the tire patterns and the foot prints, so when I catch them, I can prove it!" My Dad never had a more determined look on his face.

My Dad said, "I'm going to catch the rotten scoundrels that did this!"

I yelled, "Let's catch them and shoot them, just like they shot Ole Strawberry!"

My father stopped and looked toward me and said, "Son, we can't shot someone for killing a cow!"

I yelled, "Strawberry wasn't just a cow, she was my friend!"

My Dad walked over to me and got down on his knees in front of me and asked, "Do you remember what the Bonanza show was about last night?"

I looked down at the ground and said, "Yes, Ben Cartwright and his sons stopped a fellow rancher from hanging a cattle rustler."

My Dad asked, "What did Ben Cartwright say to the rancher?"

Then I replied, "He said, if you hang this man it would be murder, you must turn him over to the Sheriff."

My Dad said, "That's right son, I can't blame you for being mad. Heck, I'm mad too, but if we shoot them, we would be as sorry as them!"

I just looked at the ground and said, "I'm sorry, Dad, I guess I just lost my temper."

My Dad patted me on the head and said, "It's alright, son, now tell me everything you can remember about that black pickup.

I explained, "It was a black Ford about the same model as ours and it had white wall tires, red wheels and little shiny silver hub caps." As I talked, my Dad kept writing on his pad.

Then, he asked about the occupants. "Did you get a look at them?"

I just shook my head and said, "No sir, it was too dark and they were moving too fast.

My Dad stands up and looks at his writing pad and says, "Well, we know that there were two of them, they drink Old Harper's whiskey, they were wearing boots, we know what they were driving and we know they had a gun."

Then I added, "And they have a cow bell and a belt with 'Ole Strawberry' on it!"

Dad said, "Yes, I guess they do, but I just don't understand why people get drunk and do such stupid, senseless things!"

I looked up at the buzzards circling overhead and said, "Dad, please don't let the buzzards eat 'Ole Strawberry'. Can we dig a grave for her?"

My Dad just shook his head and said, "She's way too big for a grave, but we can get some shovels and mound dirt on top of her, if you want to."

Then I asked, "Can I put some stones around the mound to mark the spot?"

My Father said, "Sure son, if you want to, but first I need to go get the shovels and call the Sheriff, so he can write up a report and post a look-out for the hoodlums and their black truck."

I walked back to our car and retrieved my Red Rider BB gun and said, "I'm going to stay here while you go to call the Sheriff and keep the buzzards from landing!" I don't think my Father liked the thought of leaving me there but he knew I wanted to do this for Ole Strawberry.

As my Dad drove away, I realized Ole Strawberry had been more of a pet than a cow. I just couldn't understand how somebody could be so cruel as to kill a friendly, gentle animal like 'Ole Strawberry'.

The Sheriff came and filled out a report and then called a look-out for the hoodlums and their black pick up. After the Sheriff left, my Dad and I spent about an hour mounding dirt on top of 'Ole Strawberry' and I spent the rest of the afternoon placing stones around the mound.

On Monday morning my Dad drove to the liquor store about 35 miles away, the nearest place to us that sold hard liquor and questioned the owners. One of the owners said he remembered two men in a black pick up buying Old Harper's, but didn't know their names. My Father left his phone number and asked him to call him, if they showed up again.

Over the next week, my Dad personally visited every law enforcement office in all the surrounding counties looking for Strawberry's killers. Several officers remembered seeing a black pick up with white wall tires and red wheels and said they would keep an eye out for them.

The next week I started back to school and I told my teacher about what happened to Ole Strawberry and she let me tell the class what happened. Many of the other students lived on farms and had cows so I wanted to tell them the story.

Another week passed and early one Sunday morning a Sheriff's car entered our driveway and parked in front of our home. My Father recognized the man as the Sheriff from a county just south of us. Dad walked out the front door to speak to the man and I followed him. The Sheriff shook hands with my Dad and explained he had something to show my Dad. As the Sheriff walked to the rear of his car, he explained that a tragic accident had occurred just after midnight. Two young men driving a black Ford pick-up, at a very high rate of speed, had failed to make a curve on Old Mill Pond Road, near the China Hill community. He explained they hit a tree after leaving the road and both the driver and passenger were killed.

As the Sheriff continued to talk, he removed a paper sack from the trunk of his car and said, "They were both heavily intoxicated and I found an Old Harper's whiskey bottle in the wreckage." Then he pulls an old .38 caliber pistol from the sack and says, "This gun has three spent shells in the cylinder." Then the Sheriff reaches back into the bag and says, "I thought this might be of interest to you."

The Sheriff pulled a leather belt and brass bell from the bag and turned it over to reveal the words 'Ole Strawberry' engraved on the side and then handed it to my Dad. The Sheriff said, "This was hanging from what was left of the rear view mirror."

My Dad just shook his head and said, "I didn't mean for it to end this way, I just wanted to put them in jail!"

The Sheriff nods his head in agreement and says, "I'm sorry it happened this way, but I guess this closes your case."

My Father said, "Thank you for returning the bell and coming to tell us what happened!" My Father shook the Sheriff's hand again and he drove away.

My Father looked very sad as he said, "I didn't want anything like this to happen, son!"

I looked up at him and said, "I know!"

He handed me the bell and said, "I'm going to give this to you!"

I said, "Thanks, Dad, but I'm going to give it back to Ole Strawberry."

I put the leather belt that held the bell over the handle of my bike and peddled across the road and around the country store and down the dirt road, across the railroad tracks and on to the rock bordered mound. I parked my bike and walked over to the mound of dirt and leaned over and laid the leather belt and bell on top of the mound, then I backed up a few steps and saluted and said, "Rest in peace, my fine friend!"

I then turned around and walked away rolling my bike along and I thought about how mad I was at the people that killed 'Ole Strawberry', but after their tragic accident, I felt ashamed of myself for feeling that way. Now fifty years later, the mound is much smaller, but the stones still circle 'Ole Strawberry'. She died so senselessly, but I can still see her in my dreams with her tail wagging and her bell ringing.

The House on Gresham Road

It was a pretty spring morning in May 1960. The flowers were blooming, the trees had sprouted new leaves and the grass had turned green again. My father and I was painting window screen frames for one of our rental houses under a large pine tree that sat in the middle of our circular driveway that led to our country home.

The birds were singing and the noise from the nearby highway made it difficult to hear Mom calling my Dad to the phone. Finally, we heard Mom call.

Dad laid his paint brush down and said, "Finish up for me, kid."

When your father leaves you in-charge of painting, when you are only eight years old, it gives you a feeling of pride, but Dad knew I would do a good job.

A few minutes passed before he returned with two glasses of lemonade.

He said, "Here, son, take a break and drink your lemonade."

As I sipped the lemonade, I asked, "Who was on the phone?"

My Dad said, "It was Mrs. Mamie."

I asked, "Mrs. Who?"

My father explained, "She lived in that white house just across the railroad on Gresham Road.

31

I remembered the house after Dad explained where she lived. The white house had flowers, shrubbery, and two big oak trees; one in the front yard and the other in the back yard. As I remembered the place, I also realized that it had a run-down look lately. The weeds and grass had over taken what was once a beautiful place.

Dad said, "She wants to talk to me about her house when I get a chance.

A few days went by before Dad went to see the older lady, Mrs. Mamie, at a local nursing home. When Dad talked to her, she explained that she had fallen just over a year before and when the broken hip didn't heal properly, she had to move to the nursing home. She gave my Dad a key to the house on Gresham Road and she gave him an old photograph of it taken many years before when it was new. She asked my father to give her a price to restore the old house to its original beauty and condition.

The next day after school my Dad took me with him to the old house. It was in poor condition to say the least. The front and rear steps as well as the decking boards on the porches were rotten; some had fallen in. A porch swing on the front porch had collapsed on one side. Many of the window panes were broken and the paint on the inside and outside had peeled from the wood like long sheets of paper strips.

My father shook his head in disbelief as he continued to make notations in his writing pad. As we walked around the house, we saw sheets covering old wooden furniture and in one corner, we saw a large upright piano. The sun shining in through what was left of the broken window panes showed the dust storm we were making as we walked through the old house. We saw pictures on the walls of a young couple and two children, a girl and a boy. Everything in the old house was apparently where it was the day Mrs. Mamie got hurt.

After walking, looking, and writing for nearly an hour Dad locked the door and we walked through the weeds and tall grass back to our car. Dad stopped and took one more look back toward the old house before throwing his writing pad on the dash of our car and driving away.

Several days went by before we received another call from Mrs. Mamie. I think my Dad had realized the repair bill would be much more than she could ever afford and he apparently was in no hurry to tell her the bad news. My Dad did his best to explain to her, without hurting her feelings, that the repair bill to completely remodel the house would be a lot of money.

She told my Dad she had some cash saved up and she would be willing to let my Dad rent the house afterwards and try to collect enough rent to pay off the balance.

Her life's savings was only $200.00. The materials alone would be many times that amount. It would be a financial hardship on us to take the old lady's offer, but I knew Dad would; he had a big heart.

In the days ahead, we spent many afternoons and weekends working on that old house. My Mom helped.

She worked in the flower beds, trimmed the shrubs, and washed the curtains. In a couple of months the house was beautiful again; it looked brand new!

My Dad held the picture Mrs. Mamie had given him up while in front of the house and said, "If anything, it looks even better."

One thing puzzled me; my Dad had built a wheel chair ramp on the right side of the front porch. I couldn't understand why, but you didn't argue with my Dad, because he always had a reason for everything. After the remodeling was finished, we cleaned up everything, even the door knobs sparkled.

On Sunday morning my Mom fixed a large meal of fried chicken, biscuits, gravy, mashed potatoes, butter beans and banana pudding. She put the delicious food in covered containers, placed them in a cardboard box and covered it with a folded tablecloth to keep it hot. I knew a picnic was coming. Usually, we would have picnics at our farm or at the local state park, but my Dad drove straight to the white house on Gresham Road. After Dad unloaded the box and sat it on the kitchen counter, my Dad went to get Mrs. Mamie.

As he drove along, Dad told me the story concerning Mrs. Mamie. He told me her husband, who had died before I was born, had built that house and they had raised a son and a daughter. Mrs. Mamie's husband had been crippled in a logging accident shortly after their kids were born and had spent most of his life in a wheel chair. He had tried to

34

support his family by sharpening saw blades and Mrs. Mamie did peoples laundry, baby sat the neighbor's kids, and baked and sold pies on Saturdays. He explained their son joined the army and became a lawyer, but he lived in Chicago. He explained their daughter married a sailor and moved to San Diego, California, but apparently only rarely visited their mother. He explained that apparently they didn't come to see their mother very often, because it reminded them of their humble upbringing.

When we arrived at the nursing home, I got to meet Mrs. Mamie for the first time and the first thing I noticed was her big beautiful smile. After hearing the sad story my father had just told me, I was happily surprised to see a smiling beautiful older lady with her snow-white hair rolled up in a ball and tied with a bright red ribbon. She was wearing a white dress with red buttons and was sitting in a wheel chair. Now I knew why Dad had built that ramp. We helped Mrs. Mamie get into our car and Dad put her wheel chair in the trunk.

When we arrived at her house on Gresham Road, Mrs. Mamie screamed, laughed, and cried as we pulled into the driveway and parked next to the wheel chair ramp. A crowd of people were standing on the front porch to welcome her home. Dad helped her into her wheel chair as she hugged and kissed everybody that came to see her. I realized that most of her neighbors were unaware of her accident. Most had figured she had gone to live with her children.

After enjoying the delicious meal, Mrs. Mamie took command of her wheel chair and toured the rest of the house. Even though we had repainted the walls, we had replaced all of her family pictures back on the walls where they originally hung. Mrs. Mamie's complexion changed as she looked at the pictures. Tears ran down her face. She asked us if we would please store her personal items, including the pictures of her children.

She said, "Please give them to my children after I die, and I want you to get a deed prepared so that I can deed this house to you!"

My Dad looked very shocked at what Mrs. Mamie had said.

Mrs. Mamie continued, "Please try to find a young family to sell this home to, then take out the additional repair cost."

My father said, "I'll be glad to, but just don't worry about it today; I just want you to relax and enjoy yourself today!"

It was nearly dark before we drove Mrs. Mamie back to the nursing home. We all gave her a big hug and said good bye.

The next day my father got the deed prepared and Mrs. Mamie signed it. My father had asked her before she signed the paper, if she was sure she wanted to sell the house, and she said, yes.

My father returned the picture of the house she had loaned my dad before we started the work. He also gave her a picture of the house in its current condition.

A few weeks later we received the sad news Mrs. Mamie had passed away in her sleep. We were told she had died with a smile on her face and was holding some pictures in her hand; the pictures of a young family and of the house on Gresham Road.

The Saturday afternoon funeral was held in a small white church only a short distance from Mrs. Mamie's home. I believe everybody in town turned out for her funeral. The minister said that Mrs. Mamie was a shining example of dedication, determination, strength, will power, and unselfish love. He said she washed clothes, baked and sold pies, baby sat children, and taught piano lessons to support her family after her husband's unfortunate accident that left him crippled, and still found time to play the piano in church for nearly fifty years.

He said, "I can prove she touched everybody here." Then he asked, "Please raise your hand, if she washed your family's clothes, baby sat you when you were young, or if you enjoyed one of her delicious pies."

Every person at the funeral raised their hand.

The preacher said that Mrs. Mamie and her husband both were orphans. He was left on the door steps of a church, and she was abandoned on a passenger train with a note that said, "Please find my baby a good home."

As we left the cemetery and drove up the street, we saw an old station wagon with wood on the sides parked in the driveway to Mrs. Mamie's house. We stopped to see what was going on. A young couple standing beside the car asked us if this house was for rent.

My Dad said, "Well, actually I'm supposed to sell it for an old friend."

As he said that, Dad glanced back up the street toward the cemetery. The man was about thirty years old and had a slim build. He had brown hair and wore a plaid shirt and blue jeans. The woman looked a little younger and had shoulder length black hair. She wore a flowered dress. Two kids, a boy about eight years old and a little girl about six, smiled and waved at us from the back seat of their car.

The man said, "We can't afford to buy right now; we don't have enough money."

My Dad scratched his jaw with his fingers and said, "Maybe I could arrange a payment plan you can afford."

As Dad led them toward the house, you couldn't help but notice the man had a profound limp. The man explained to us that he had an artificial leg, and that he had lost it in an automobile accident when he was a kid.

My father froze in his tracks and said, "You don't happen to sharpen saw blades, do you?"

He replied, "No, but I do have a new job inspecting the soft drink bottles for the local cola bottler."

As we approached the porch, the man walked around to the wheel chair ramp that my Dad and I thought would only be used temporarily. The man told Dad he had trouble with stairs, but the ramp was perfect.

The lady asked my Dad, if it was alright to let the kids get out, and of course, he agreed. The kids ran and yelled around the house, as my Dad unlocked the door.

The couple was very impressed, not only with the house and yard, but with the old furniture, as well. The lady noticed the piano and asked, if they could rent the house and the furnishings, as well.

The kids continued to run and play. Their mother explained that they had always lived in a boarding house in downtown Macon and had never had a yard for them to play.

The couple once again asked my Dad to please rent them the house and furnishings. My father walked over to the window and saw two of the happiest children he had ever seen playing in the yard and then he looked back to see the young couple hugging each other as they looked around the house.

My father asked, "How much money do you have?"

The man said, "We have saved up $500.00 to cover the move and to buy furniture."

My Dad looked over toward my Mom who had just followed us into the house and gave her a wink as he said, "$500.00 and the house and furniture is yours!"

The couple looked completely shocked as they stood there with their mouths and eyes wide open.

The lady asked, "Are you serious?"

My Dad said, "Yes, it's yours."

The man asked, "How can you sell this place including the furniture for only $500.00 when it's probably worth $5000.00?"

My Dad said, "I'm selling it for a friend and she wanted me to find a special family. I think you're perfect."

The couple still standing like two statues couldn't believe their ears.

The lady looked doubtful as she said, "Is this some kind of joke?"

My Dad replied, "You put $500.00 in my hand and we will record the deed on Monday morning at 9 o'clock."

The man reached for his wallet while Dad walked out to our car to get his brief case out of the trunk. My Dad wrote their names on a deed and gave them a receipt for the money.

While the men handled the paperwork, my Mom explained to the young lady that all the linens had been laundered and showed her where the pillow cases, sheets, blankets and towels were.

Dad explained that the water and power would be left on for them, if they wanted to spend the night. He told them they could change the utilities over when they got their first paycheck after they moved in.

The man explained that everything they owned was in that old station wagon parked in the driveway.

My father recorded the deed on Monday morning. Dad and Mom boxed and shipped Mrs. Mamie's personal items, family pictures, etc., to her son and daughter with a short note about why he had remodeled their mother's home and then sold it.

A week later Dad received a letter from Mrs. Mamie's daughter thanking him for granting her mom her last wish and for sending some of her mom's personal items.

The end of the year came and my father was working on his taxes when his lawyer came across the job he had done for Mrs. Mamie. The lawyer studied the facts and figures and said, "You lost a lot of money on this job!"

My Dad just grinned and said, "No, this was one of my biggest profits!"

The lawyer said, "Well, I don't see where you put it in the bank."

My Dad turned and looked at my Mom and me and said, "The best profits are the ones you deposit in your heart."

I wasn't worried about this big deposit in my Dad's heart, because I knew he had a big heart and could make room for it.

For over twenty-five years after I left home, I still returned at least one day a week to help my Father and Mother operate their farm and keep up their rental property. I never charged them a dime, but it was one of the largest profits I ever placed in my heart. I wouldn't trade anything for the extra time I spent with them. It is truly better to give, than receive.

Paying Attention

It was 1961 and I lived on a farm a few miles from a small town in South Georgia. My father had built a small country style store on the edge of the little town of Helena. Now, Helena wasn't one of those towns you got lost in, but instead it was one you got lost trying to find.

On Saturday morning I got my father to load my Western Flyer bike in the back of his pick-up for the trip to town. I wanted to ride it during the day in between helping dad run the store.

There was a little girl that lived just down the dirt street beside the Seaboard Railroad and I thought she was very pretty, brown hair, brown eyes and a pretty smile!

As soon as we opened the store, people started coming in and it was barely 7:00 a.m. The little store sat at the crossroads of two train tracks, the Southern ran north and south and the Seaboard ran east and west, and they crossed only about one hundred fifty feet from our little store.

Several times a day, trains came and went and the people seemed to just ignore the noise and go about their lives. In the background was the turpentine still. All day long farmers brought large wooden barrels of pine tar to the still. A large water tank stood on the south side of the Seaboard railway and I always wanted to climb it to the top. Thankfully, I never got around to that or else I probably wouldn't be here to write this story.

On this bright sunny June morning I decided to ride my bike down the dirt road that ran by the railroad to do a little showing off for the pretty little girl with the brown hair that I knew from school. I rode by a couple of times, but I didn't seem to get her attention. The only attention I seem to get was from her small brown and white dog. I wasn't one to give up easy, so I decided to go up the hill and ride down it balancing myself while standing on the seat and using my out stretched arms for balance. I figured this would get her attention.

So away I went, picking up a little speed, I eased up on my feet, balancing as I stood on the seat, but when I looked away to see if I was getting her attention, Crash, Bang, Boom, Ouch! I had crashed to the ground with my shiny new bike on top of me, the shiny chrome spokes glittering in the sunlight as the front wheel continued to turn directly above my face.

I was still trying to figure out what had caused such a crash when her dog ran out barking and licked my face. Well, at least I had gotten some attention, but not quite what I had in mind.

The next thing I saw was her dad standing over me. "Are you alright, young fellow?" he asked.

"Sure, I'm fine," I said as I finally managed to recoup enough breath to speak.

Now that I think about it this was my first attempt to impress a girl and perform bike surfing at the same time.

The kind man lifted the bike off of me, made the dog leave me alone, and helped me to my feet. My elbow was bleeding a little from the collision, but other than dirtying up my face and hurt feelings, I was fine. The bike hadn't fared as well. The handle bars were turned sideways, so the kind man loaded it up in his pick-up and gave me a ride back to our store.

After we arrived at the store, my father came out and after explaining to him that I had an accident on my bike, he laughed and thanked the man.

He then introduced him to me and said, "He's you mother's cousin's son."

I asked, "Was the pretty little brown haired girl his daughter?"

And he nodded, "Yes, she is."

Now I think they knew what had happened.

Then I recognized this man as one of the men that operated the turpentine still. He had told me he was the one that pulled the whistle every day at noon. My father thanked the man again.

As he drove away my father told me that it wasn't proper for cousin's to date or marry and I needed to look further. I wasn't planning on dating her or marrying her. I was only ten years old, but I guessed I just wanted a little attention.

I was one of six kids raised in the country. My older brothers were too old to have anything to do with me. My sister was too mean and of course she was a girl and my little brother was too young. We had no neighbors. I was ugly, red-headed, and had a face full of freckles, not to mention an ugly birthmark on the left side of my face. I should have known better. I was so ugly and she was so pretty. Well, at least I had made friends with her dad and her dog.

As the years went by, I would speak to her at school and think about what my dad had said. Every time I heard that whistle blow at noon time I would think of this fine man and of course his beautiful little daughter.

Years later I did everything you could think of with a car, but stand on top of it to impress women, but I always remembered where it all began, on a dirt road in Helena that ran down by the railroad tracks.

Starliner

In 1961, we lived in the county, five miles north of Helena. We had a farm with a few cows. I remember one that was white with red spots. We called it the "Strawberry" cow, but enough about cows. It was "new car" time. My dad had announced that "new car" fever had struck and he wanted a "new car."

My three older brothers, all teenagers, were salivating at the thought. Now what usually happens is people remember the prices from several years ago and sort of assume the prices are still the same and of course, pigs fly.

On Saturday afternoon, we rode to town to see the new cars. Now I was the most car crazy ten year old on Earth. I wasn't old enough to be "girl crazy" yet, but with a farm and several rental houses to paint, I didn't have much time to get involved in anything else. I lived, ate, slept, and dreamed about cars. I knew every model and year and style even the engines, trim, hub caps, and where the antenna was supposed to be.

We stopped at the Ford lot. I couldn't wait for the door to open, out I ran to look in the showroom. Wow! A red Thunderbird convertible sat there, but even a dumb ten year old knew that wasn't practical for a family of eight, so reality set in and we walked around the lot. My dad was suddenly struck by sticker shock, same thing at the Chevy dealer, then on to the Dodge lot.

While walking through the Dodge lot, I thought this must be a bad year for Dodge. I just didn't really like any of them.

Then my dad called to us, "Look, here's one we could afford."

There in front of me was probably one of the ugliest cars I had ever seen in my life. It's a straight shift and overdrive, just what I wanted. Oh no, not the "just what I wanted" line. That was the "just what I wanted" line I was taught to say to anyone that gave me anything, whether it would be Christmas or birthday or whatever. Back then we country kids didn't get a whole lot of stuff like they do now. We were grateful for whatever we did get, but I hoped my dad would forget about this big, ugly, white Dodge and go back to see the Ford or Chevy.

Several days went by. Dad picked me up after school to help him on the farm, but first a quick stop at Dennis Cleaners. Rudolph Dennis, the owner, was one of dad's best friends. If he told me once, he told me a thousand times, what a fine man he was. Oh no, right next door, you guessed it, was the Dodge place and right in front of us was that ugly white Dodge. Maybe dad won't notice, but he did.

"Come on kid, let's get the keys and take it for a ride," dad said.

My dad walked right inside the Griffith's Motor Company showroom and retrieved the keys to this dismal looking car. I thought about it. This car must have been designed by a drunk as a joke and some idiot got the plans mixed up by mistake and actually built this horrid looking automotive monster.

Well, it was new and sitting inside it didn't look as ugly as we sped out of the dealership parking lot. Maybe buzzards would attack or a big dog would bury this thing in somebody's backyard. Anything would be an improvement.

Aw! The smell, there's nothing like the smell of a new car. I believe to this day that car manufacturers have treated new cars with some sort of chemical narcotic that will cause people to loose complete control, throw common sense to the wind, and plunge head-long in to years of payments.

Maybe this car wasn't so bad after all. Then suddenly, I saw our reflection in a store window. Yuk! That car looked like a car from hell. The only thing it needed was flames.

A few days went by and on Friday, Dad didn't come home in time for supper. Mom told us he was going to be late, because he was bringing home a new car.

She looked straight at me and said, "We are all going to be pleased and happy, do you understand."

"Yes, Mom," I replied.

What a bummer. I lay on the floor face down like a slug. I loved my father and didn't want to hurt his feelings.

What can I possibly say? Could I possibly think of something good?

If I said, "Wow, dad, it's beautiful," He would know I was lying.

Then suddenly, it hit me. Even the ugliest car on Earth smelled good! No sooner than I stood up relieved that I had thought of something good to say about the Frankenstein of all cars, I felt better. You know as ugly as this car was, maybe other kids would feel sorry for me and stop picking on me for being so ugly.

"I'd rather be dead than red on the head." If I'd heard that once, I had heard that a thousand times.

Suddenly, I saw the headlights coming up the big circular driveway to our home. Well, this is it. Try to keep a straight face. Don't hurt dad's feelings. March out that front door with the white swan on it and go look at the ugly duckling.

Coming to a sudden stop on our gravel drive, I looked up slowly, but the ugly white car was nowhere to be seen. Instead my 6'4' tall dad stepped out of the most beautiful car I had ever seen in my life. It was absolutely beautiful, black, lots of chrome, a fastback roof that looked more like a spaceship than a car. The red and white interior glowed under the overhead light like strawberries and whipped cream. F-O-R-D Starliner on the side plate. I couldn't believe my eyes. So many tears of joy were running down my face. It's a wonder I didn't slip down.

I was prepared for the ugly duckling and instead a beautiful swan appeared. This was one of the most beautiful special edition cars ever built even to this day. I bit my hand just to be sure I wasn't dreaming.

This taught me a powerful lesson. Never give up and maybe the ugly ducklings you're expecting will become beautiful swans.

Goat Man Story

We lived on a farm that stretched along US 341 Highway between Achord and Jay Bird Springs in Dodge County, Georgia. Once a year we came under attack from the North! No, not Yankees, I'm talking about the Goat Man.

Now, for those of you fortunate enough not to know who the Goat Man was, I'll explain. This was a man who lived in an old school bus body in Twiggs County near Jeffersonville, Georgia, with a bunch of goats! Every year, usually during the Spring or Fall, this man would hook up about a dozen goats to the most obnoxious looking wagon, it looked like a junkyard on wheels, and strike out for Coastal Georgia.

Now my Dad didn't like the Goat Man and just the mention of his name would raise my Dad's blood pressure 30 points.

Some people said the Goat Man with his long hair and even longer shabby beard looked like a goat and smelled like a goat.

My Dad disagreed. He said, "The goats were much prettier."

Now we were timber farmers and had several hundred acres of good pine timber. We actually used some of our timber to build houses and we also sold turpentine. For you city slickers, you get turpentine from pine tar. Timber was important to us and we treated our trees like family.

When the Goat Man traveled, he always seemed to stop along the highway on some of our property. When the Goat Man camped out on your property, they destroyed everything on it, like an attack from locust. Goats would even eat the bark off of young pine trees, killing hundreds of young trees, costing us lots of money. It seemed like the Goat Man would pick some of the most beautiful places along the highways to annihilate!

Late one Saturday afternoon as we returned from a day at the beach, our day was destroyed when we turned in our driveway and saw the Goat Man camped out on our property.

My father had warned the Goat Man repeatedly not to camp out on our property, but there he was in front of our home.

Dad hit the brakes so hard in our new Ford car that all four Firestone tires screeched to a halt. Dad grabbed his 38 Smith and Wesson from the glove box and said, "That's it. I'm going to shoot that Goat Man and his stinking goats!"

My Mom pleaded with my Dad and reminded him he was being a bad example in front of the kids!

At 6 foot, 4 inches tall and 285 pounds, my Dad didn't really need a gun. Dad walked up to the Goat Man and yelled, "Get off of my property before I strangle you and those stupid goats!"

The Goat Man verbally protested, but quickly harnessed the goats to his wagon and left. As the Goat Man pulled his goat wagon out on the highway heading north he yelled, "It's getting dark and if a car hits us, it's going to be your fault."

My Dad yelled, "I'd only feel sorry for the car!"

On Sunday morning the sun was shining, the birds were singing, as we ate breakfast and got dressed for church. I was hoping my Father had forgotten about his encounter with the Goat Man the night before. Everything was fine as we pulled out of our driveway heading north for the one mile to our church.

As we approached our church, cars were parked on both sides of the road for as far as you could see.

My Dad was concerned. He thought, "What's going on, a car wreck, or fire, or what could cause all of these people to park along the sides of the road."

As we approached the entrance to our little white country church, I couldn't believe my eyes. Parked right out front on our church's nice, neatly mowed grass parking lot was, you guessed it, the Goat Man, trailer, and goats!

My Mom yells, "Oh, no." Then she reminds my Dad about his blood pressure, us kids in the car, and the fact we were in front of our church.

My Dad stepped on the throttle as we pulled into the parking area.

I thought, "My Dad is going to run over the Goat Man, goats, and junky wagon." But he stopped our Ford

Starliner about six inches from the wagon and he hit the horn button for several seconds and then got out of the car.

Dad just folded his big arms across his chest and stared at the Goat Man.

I don't think I've ever seen anybody move as fast as the Goat Man as he called his goats by name and hooked them up to the wagon. He was gone in about sixty seconds.

My Father then turned around and faced the dozens of people who were standing in line to give the Goat Man a dollar to take a picture of him and his goats. They all quickly walked back to their cars and left.

The pastor and some of the other church members who had arrived earlier walked up to Dad.

The pastor says, "I can't believe it. We begged and pleaded for him to leave and he paid us no mind, but he left quickly for you, even though you didn't say a word!"

My Mom walked up to my Dad and she put her arm around him and said, "Maybe he just read your mind!"

After her comment, everybody started laughing and we never saw the Goat Man again.

For years afterwards we heard stories about the Goat Man going to Texas, California, or even Canada, but we never saw him again. Who knows, maybe he really did read my Dad's mind.

A Rose for Miss Winnie

(Mail Order Bride)

It was mid-afternoon on a fall day in Helena, Georgia as I, a twelve year old boy, was busy helping my father put the finishing touches on a new house on Cemetery Road. As I mounted the fasteners for the window screens, I suddenly realized someone was standing behind me.

As I turned to look, I realized it was an upper fifties man who lived next door in a small concrete block house. I had never seen this man so dressed up before. He was wearing a coat and tie and was holding a single rose in a small round holder in his right hand. I waited a moment for the man to speak, but he did not, so I asked, "Can I help you, sir?"

The man finally spoke and said, "I need to speak to your father."

I replied, "He is inside installing the handles on the cabinets." as I pointed to the window.

The man just stood there motionless for a few seconds, so I said, "I will get him for you." I walked inside and told my Dad, "Mr. Marvin from next door wants to speak to you, Dad."

My Dad laid down his screwdriver and followed me outside. Dad saw the man still standing where I left him and gave me a strange look. I do not think my Dad had ever seen this man wearing anything, but work clothes, much less holding a rose in his hand. My Dad said, "Hi, Marvin. What can I do for you?"

The man suddenly glanced up at my Dad and said, "I want to get married!"

My Dad just laughed and said, "I cannot help you. I am already married!"

The man's face suddenly turned red as he blushed and said, "No, I am going to meet my bride on the 3:00 o'clock bus from Macon and I want you to introduce me to her."

My Dad gave a puzzled look as he asked, "How am I going to introduce you to her when I don't know who she is?"

The man spoke up, "She will be wearing a yellow dress and a hat with flowers on it."

My Dad still had a puzzled look on his face as he asked, "Are you serious. You are going to marry a woman you have never met."

Marvin did not answer. He just nodded his head in the affirmative.

The man had never been married. He had lived next door with his mother until she died a few months before. Apparently he had written a letter to a lonely hearts club sponsored by a church in Macon and asked for help to locate a wife. The pastor of the church had given the letter to an upper 50's woman who for many years had been caretaker of the church and its grounds in trade for room and board. The woman had never been married and had no family. The pastor figured this would make a good match.

As my Dad and the man stood there, I looked at my wrist watch and said, "It is almost 3:00 o'clock."

The man almost jumped as I spoke. You could tell he was nervous. The man cleared his throat and said, "I am a little nervous. Would you mind driving me to the bus station to meet Miss Winnie, then on to the courthouse?"

My Dad smiled and said, "Sure, I would be glad to help out!"

On the way to the bus station the man talked about how lonely he had been since his mother died and about how this woman, Miss Winnie, loved flowers and could take care of his mother's many flower beds. He said he told her he would be holding a single rose when she got off of the bus. As we arrived at the bus station, the Macon bus pulled in right behind us as Dad parked our car behind the station.

When the man exited our car, I pointed out that his shoes were untied. He quickly handed the small container holding the rose to my Dad as he bent over to tie his shoes.

Suddenly, the door of the bus opened and an older lady wearing a yellow dress and a hat with flowers on it came rushing down the steps and yelled, "My dear Marvin, I would know you anywhere." Then she wrapped her arms around my Dad.

I think my Dad was in shock as he handed the small container with the rose in it to Marvin who had just finished tying his shoes. My Dad finally muttered the words, "He is Marvin."

The lady then turned my Dad loose and wrapped her arms around the man and said, "My dear Marvin, I would know you anywhere." As the lady held tight to Marvin, my Dad's face showed signs of relief!

I guess even though my Dad was 20 years younger and 100 pounds heavier, he was holding a single rose. It was just a simple mistake.

After just a few minutes of conversation, my Dad suggested we get to the courthouse for the ceremony. As we entered the courthouse, we could tell that something special was about to happen. A table had been set up in the large foyer and paper plates, cups, napkins, and a big punch bowl were arranged for some special event. Apparently the courthouse officials and their staff had decided to welcome the new citizen to Telfair County southern style.

As we closed the big door behind us, about a dozen people including the sheriff, entered the foyer to greet the couple. The sheriff who had been injured in the line of duty was in his wheelchair with his arms reaching out to hug Miss Winnie.

A lady entered carrying a white cake with a wedding couple figurine on top and sat it on the table. She smiled and turned to walk away when the sheriff said, "Stay for the ceremony."

The young lady continued to smile as she said, "Oh, I better get back to the bakery before my boss fires me."

The sheriff replied, "If he does, I will put him in jail."

Everybody laughed and the young lady said, "Well, maybe for a few minutes."

The judge was the last person to arrive and he performed the ceremony in just a couple of minutes. He then shook hands with Marvin, hugged Miss Winnie's neck, and left as quickly as he arrived.

It suddenly occurred to me that just a few minutes earlier, I was installing screens on a ladder and now I am eating cake and having punch at a wedding.

One of the elected officials offered to take them to a restaurant and buy them a steak dinner when another official spoke up and said, "I out rank you, so I get to take them out to eat."

One of the ladies in the group says, "Are you gentlemen trying to buy the vote of our newest citizen?"

They both answered in unison, "Yes."

Everybody in the foyer was laughing at the response.

My Dad whispered, "Son, we have work to finish."

My Dad and I wished the couple many great years together and then we left.

Over the next twenty five years, even after I graduated from high school, went to college, started my own business in Warner Robins, married a young lady from Cochran, and started a family of my own, I still came back home to help my parents with their farm and rental property, at least one day a week.

On those days, many times I would ride by the simple little white block house on Cemetery Road and see Marvin and Miss Winnie working in the flower beds, garden, or just rocking in their rocking chairs on the front porch of their little home. I would blow the horn in my pickup and wave at them and they always stood up and waved back at me.

Then one day Marvin drove his faded old pickup truck to town to get some bone meal for Miss Winnie's rose bushes and returned to find Miss Winnie had passed away in her favorite rocking chair on their front porch. She had died with a smile on her face and in her hands was the letter Marvin had mailed to her all those years before in which he asked her to marry him.

Marvin had Miss Winnie buried in the cemetery at the top of the hill near his mother's grave. He left one open spot between them, because he wanted to be buried in between the two women he loved.

A few days went by and the monument company that had just installed the granite slab on Miss Winnie's grave stopped by to tell Mr. Marvin that the job was completed.

The next morning Marvin walked to Miss Winnie's grave and placed a single rose in the same glass holder he was holding the day he first met her.

A note attached to the rose said, "To my beautiful, darling Miss Winnie, on the day we met, I gave you a rose, and you gave me your heart. Here's one last rose before we part!"

McRae-Helena Treasure Hunt

In 1965 the McRae-Helena merchants got tired of
seeing its citizens shopping in Vidalia, Dublin, and
Douglas, so they came up with a plan to keep them home.
They called it the "McRae-Helena Treasure Hunt." A
small treasure chest was hidden somewhere in the adjoining
towns and the lucky person who found it would receive
cash and prizes donated by the local merchants totaling
over $1000.00. In today's money that is approximately
$10,000.00-$12,000.00.

The local radio personality, Ira Caldwell, would give
two clues a day concerning the whereabouts of the hidden
treasure. People stayed glued to their radios much like
those dogs on the RCA Victor logo of the day. Every week
the Telfair Enterprise would recap the week's clues and
wish the treasure hunters good luck in the hunt. It got to
the point that shoppers from Vidalia, Dublin, and Douglas
were shopping in the McRae-Helena stores, so they could
try to find the elusive treasure. Eventually, people as far
away as Macon joined the search after the Macon Evening
News ran a story on the treasure hunt.

Some of the clues were, "You can hear cars starting and
stopping, people walking and talking." Clues also
included, "It is not on the ground, it is not indoors, and it is
protected from the sun and rain."

The contest became the number one topic of discussion
as people exchanged their thoughts on the treasure
locations. As the contest continued, people were looking in

trash cans, behind park benches, in phone booths, under cars, in tree houses, and everywhere else a small metal box could be hidden.

After several months some people began to complain and said, "It is probably a hoax! Maybe there is no hidden treasure!"

The merchants assured the public that the contest was real!

A new clue came out one Saturday morning that said, "If the treasure chest had a nose, it would smell something wonderful."

About mid-afternoon, a teenage boy working part-time at a store in McRae decides to walk down the street to Harbins Hamburgers for a little snack. For only 25 cents you could get "the special" which was a small hamburger in a sack with some batter dipped fries and a bottle of Coke.

As he walked down Railroad Street, he was daydreaming about a car he wanted to buy. He had already found a great deal at Selph's Used Cars. It was a plain black 2-door Plymouth with a big V-8 engine, better known as a former Pennsylvanian state patrol car. The salesman, Mr. Howard, had cut the price to only $500.00, not bad for a three year old car, but it needed new tires, brakes, a complete service job, and the radiator was bad, as well as the battery. But to a teenage boy approaching the magic 16th birthday, this car was excitement on wheels. He realizes that he may not be able to get the $500.00 for the car before someone else buys it.

As the teenager starts up the steps to Harbin's Hamburgers, he is confronted by a shabby dressed man with a week old beard, probably a hobo who had been sleeping it off in one of the empty rail cars parked on the side track, beside the railroad depot. He tells the teenager he is hungry and says that he has not had anything to eat for a couple of days. The teenager tells the hobo to sit down on a bench out front of the little hamburger place and to wait.

After the teenager enters the hamburger place, he counts his money. As he places the order, he only has enough for one meal. As he exits the hamburger shop and hands the food to the hobo, the teenager thinks, "Who am I kidding. I am never going to get the money to buy that car!"

As the teen turns to walk away, the hobo attacks the sack containing the food like a wild bear. The traffic light changes and a brand new blue and white 2-door Dodge car stops right in front of him.

The hobo finally manages to yell, "Thank you."

The man driving the Dodge is Mr. Griffith, the owner of Griffith's Motor Company, the local Dodge dealer. He turns the radio volume up as a new clue comes out over the radio. The DJ says, "The treasure chest is sitting on top of something that only makes a noise during the summer."

The teenager who for several weeks believed the treasure was near this very intersection turns around and races back up the steps and reaches up on top of the air conditioner and finds a small metal box. He quickly opens it to find a note that says, "Congratulations, you are the winner of the McRae-Helena treasure chest!" At the bottom of the note it says this certificate can be redeemed at the mayor's office at McRae City Hall between 8:00 a.m. and 5:00 p.m., Monday through Friday!

As he stuffs the box under his shirt and walks away, he sees several people racing toward the air conditioner unit, desperately searching for the treasure chest.

On Monday morning this fine teenager turned in the certificate and received $500.00 and purchased the black Plymouth of his dreams. Some of the other prizes included a new set of tires from Frank Reigers Service Station in Helena and a complete auto tune-up and service from Pitts Garage. A certificate from Western Auto paid for a new battery. Brooks Auto Parts supplied a new radiator. Hunt Brothers Auto Parts' share of the treasure supplied a new set of seat covers and floor mats, and last but not least, Stephens Texaco's Gift certificate was for $50.00 worth of gasoline, over 150 gallons!

This teenager's act of generosity cost him a hamburger, but if he had ignored the hungry drifter and had eaten the food at the counter, he would not have won the car. This fine example of a teenager was Shelton Young.

Unfortunately, he died about a year ago from complications from heart surgery. My wife, Brenda and I attended his funeral at Cross Point Baptist Church in Perry. I thought that one of the speakers would tell the story, but no one did!

As we left the church service, I wished I could tell everybody in America, especially teenagers, this story of a teenager's generosity and the reward that he received.

Cookie Caper!

It was 1966, yes, three years before men from Earth landed on the moon. I was a ninth grade student at Telfair County High School in McRae.

My favorite subjects were lunch and lunch. The evening break came in as a close second. Now break as we called it in high school was what kids called recess in grammar school. It was between 2:00 and 2:15 p.m. when all the inmates or I mean students dropped all their boring books, pencils, pens, pads, maps, charts, etc. and walked outside.

Now oddly enough we had just acquired a new principal. I remember to this day how I shuddered when someone told me the new principal was meaner than a bulldog and of course red headed. Now everyone knows red- headed people have a bad temper that is, all of them, except me, of course.

This new principal made a bunch of new rules, as if we needed more. I remember the only thing you could do without asking permission was breathe and look, just what we needed was more rules.

We marched to the gym for the new warden, I mean principal, to introduce himself and to unload on us all those new rules and regulations, etc. This guy just went on and on and on and on.

All of a sudden, I was awakened by "and no student can re-enter the halls during the break period."

What! No more sneaking down the hall to eat fresh baked cookies in the Home Economics class! What a monster! What a cold hearted evil, mean, rotten, no good, scoundrel could have thought of something as diabolical as not entering the halls during the evening break. All those delicious cookies were going to waste.

Every time it seems like you get even remotely use to all that junk you have to cope with to graduate from school, you get side-winded by a new principal from Hell and 3000 rules. I told myself I was going to hate this guy!

One day went by, no cookies; two days went by, no cookies, three days, no way. Now I couldn't take it anymore. Could I change one of my stupid classes at mid-term and start taking Home Economics? How would I look wearing an apron? No way. I would be hounded to the end of the Earth. I must come up with a plan. That's what I needed. I needed a plan.

There I was staring down the main hall with all those cookies, only 40 to 50 yards away.

I heard someone behind me say, "It's the cookies, isn't it?

I turned to see a guy we called Lumpy standing behind me. Now Lumpy wasn't the smartest person in the world, but I was no Einstein myself. An ally in a cookie raid didn't have to have brilliance, just an overwhelming desire to gobble up a quick dozen or so cookies.

With the big hall door open, I could smell those delicious cookies, just out of the reach of our paws, but not from my nostrils. I think these must be my favorite oatmeal, cinnamon, and brown sugar cookies, to be exact.

Lumpy said, "I'll watch for you, if you'll bring me some."

Now I realize that this is the biggest sucker scam of a plan. I'm taking all the risk.

"No way," I said. "Either we go together or the deal is off."

So down the hall we looked once more and away we went; besides aren't rules made to be broken! As we rounded the corner, we had arrived at cookies heaven. I thought to myself, all those delicious cookies and only two hands.

As the cookies slid across the cookie sheet, I heard footsteps in the hall. It was probably another brave buccaneer who decided to join the daring daylight raid. Doolittle himself would have been proud. No time to waste, the steps were getting closer. I'm getting out of here quick. Lumpy followed close behind.

Turning the corner, there he was, the devil himself. Nowhere to run, it was too late. I quickly shoved about a dozen cookies into each pocket of my jeans. I developed a lump in my throat bigger than a football. My brain was racing. What could we do to get out of this one? Why did

I let Lumpy of all people talk a darling like myself into such a clear violation of the new rules?

"Stop right there," he shouted.

This guy was angry. I turned around to Lumpy, who by now had ran into me from behind and I whispered, "He's new. Just give him somebody else's name," I said with a quick wink.

This makes all the difference between amateur cookie rustlers and the professionals.

This angry red headed and now red faced man standing in front of us was pulling out his note pad. Oh no, not a principal that tots a note pad. A principal that tots a note pad must be against the Geneva Agreement.

"What is your name?" he asked as he pointed at me.

His eyes were like lasers. Wait a minute. Were lasers invented, yet? I'm not sure. I saw one of those B-grade horror movies once, "School teachers from Hell," or something. Wasn't he in that movie? My stomach tightened. I drew a short breath. I had never felt this way before.

"John Smith, Sir," I blurted out.

This guy wrote on that pad without even looking at what he wrote. He must surely be from the dark place of fire. Now he was pointing at Lumpy. I winked at Lumpy once again trying to remind him to give the principal somebody else's name.

71

I could see the horror in his face. He was shaking. He was trembling. How did all this happen just for a few cookies? Would he burn us at the stake, or march us in front of a firing squad? Bang! Maybe he would let us go! This was our first offence today, anyway.

"Come on Lumpy, speak up you dummy. Speak up," I was shouting silently.

Finally I saw the corners of his mouth start to move like the facial expression of the Grinch who stole Christmas, and out it came.

"Gary Brown, Sir," he said.

What! This idiot gave him my name. How rotten, how stupid could he be? He gave the principal from Hell my name. How could he be so dumb?

That football in my throat became a Buick. He wrote down our names, and then he told us to report to his office at 3:15 sharp right after school.

Just as we cleared the hall, I grabbed Lumpy around the neck.

"You moron, why did you give him my name"? I asked.

His lips turned pale and he uttered, "You said give him somebody else's name. Under all that pressure, yours was the only name I could think of."

"Remind me to kill you later," I snapped as the bell rang to return to our classes.

I don't remember a thing that happened in sixth period. All I was thinking was how I got into such a jam. I remember the teacher up at the board. Blah, Blah, Blah. I didn't hear a word. I was thinking how are you going to get out of this fix? Wait a minute; thinking got me into this jam to start with.

By 3:15 I had more knots in my stomach than 3000 square foot of knotty pine paneling. What was I going to do? I could run away to Mexico. Heck, I can't speak Spanish. I murder English bad enough. Maybe I could be kidnapped by goat herders. Well it's too late. Here comes Lumpy down the hall.

"Well, are you ready to face the music?" I asked.

"He doesn't have my name. I figured he won't remember me. I'm going home," Lumpy remarked, and out the door he marched.

Could this be real? I got shafted by Lumpy. This kid was so dumb he couldn't pass a urine test, but he had cut me down like a toothpick.

I marched down the hall and reached out and turned the knob leading into the principal's office and there right in front of me was the towering inferno himself.

"Where's the other guy that was with you?" he asked.

Suddenly, a light bulb popped on in my little tiny brain.

"Sir, it grieves me so to have to inform you that the other guy with me is a liar! His name isn't John Smith. His real name is Blah Blah, better known as Lumpy," I responded.

I'll never forget the look on this guy's face. It changed. Was he going to smile as he killed me? He reached out. Was he going to strangle me? I'm too young to die; besides I'm going to get my driver's license in a few weeks. I got it; he's going to smash my head up beside the concrete block wall like a cantaloupe.

"I'm proud of you," he said. At least you came, because of your honesty and integrity. I'm going to let you off. Blah, Blah is going to get a triple dose of what the two of you would have gotten."

I stood there like a stick stuck in the mud. I couldn't believe my ears as he put his arm across my back and walked me to the door.

"I'm glad there are still some good kids left. You may go," he said as he motioned for me to leave.

I walked slowly thinking this must be a trick. He's going to shoot me in the back.

I turned and looked as the door closed behind me. Then relief, that Buick left my throat. I started breathing again. Whew! That was close. Say that was pretty cool. That ole monster actually smiled at me as he opened the door!

Then believe it or not, a tiny microscopic ting of guilt developed inside my chest. If I was a real man, I should go back in that door, march right up to our new principal and tell him the truth!

Suddenly, I remembered I wasn't a man, I was only 15. I threw the pocket full of cookies in the trash can and walked on.

Well, Lumpy never spoke to me again. Who cares? Who would want to speak to someone that dumb? Good Grief! Besides, I was only a couple of weeks away from getting my driver's license!

A Mag-nificent Dilemma

It was the final weeks before my graduation and the cash and presents were pouring in. I finally had the money to buy a beautiful set of mag wheels for my metallic gold Mustang GT. I knew my Mustang was already the most beautiful car on earth, but with mag wheels, I figured it would be even more beautiful!

One Friday morning when I arrived at school I was talking to my car, "Well, tomorrow, my little pony, you will have a brand new set of mag wheels!"

When I walked through the door of one of the most dilapidated high schools in the United States, I saw several of my fellow seniors huddled together in deep despair. I was told that Jim, one of our fellow seniors, house had burned down during the night, and his family had lost everything! To make matters worse, the house was rented and they had no insurance on their furniture or possessions. When I thought it couldn't get worst, it did. Apparently, Jim's father had hurt his back and hadn't worked in months.

A young lady, with tears running down her face, said, "Jim even lost his graduation presents!"

There I was only 24 hours away from a beautiful set of mag wheels and a little guilt slipped upon me. I tried to fight back the words, but they fell out of my mouth, "Why don't we give Jim and his family our graduation presents and cash!"

Instantly, the frowns on the students' faces became smiles. The young ladies hugged my neck and the guys slapped me on my back.

Suddenly, a little tinge of selfishness returned to my mind as I thought, "Why in the heck did I say that!"

Just that quick, I lost four shirts, two ties, five sets of handkerchiefs, six pairs of socks, a wrist watch, a college edition Webster's dictionary, a sweater with a little green lizard on the front, and $120.00 in cash.

Well, on Saturday, rather than going after my heart's desire mag wheels, I used my Dad's pickup to haul furniture, appliances, canned food, cooking utensils, and mountains of linens to a house, right behind the school.

After the town's people heard about the sacrifice we seniors had taken, everybody joined in and by dark we had completely furnished a house donated to the family for six months by a local realtor.

I must admit I was impressed with the people in this little small South Georgia town. We had lived in this little town since the beginning of the school year and I was a little homesick! I hadn't made much effort to make friends with the people, but I was impressed with the way they all worked together to help a family in need.

My father had been a little suspicious and wasn't exactly happy about me giving away all of my presents and cash.

On the Friday night before our Sunday afternoon graduation, the phone rang. One of my older brothers had told someone who had the exact mag wheels on his Mustang the story about me helping the family in need instead of buying the mag wheels.

The young man replied, "I'll gladly give him these fancy mag wheels for his stock GT wheels! He continued, "My wife and I are expecting twins. We live on a bumpy road and these wheels may be pretty, but they make a car ride terrible."

I couldn't believe my ears, but I got up early the next morning and drove about a hundred miles to meet this man at a service station in Warner Robins, Georgia. He even insisted on paying to have the wheels swapped.

I couldn't believe it. Even though I had given the money I had saved to buy the mag wheels of my heart's desire away, I still got the wheels.

I was more convinced than ever that I now owned the most beautiful metallic gold GT Mustang on earth. I found myself parking my car so that I could see the side view as I returned so that I could admire those beautiful wheels.

It was almost a year later on a weekend visit home that my father laid the small town newspaper in my lap and walked on by without saying a word. I was reading a college edition Sociology book, but the newspaper got my attention.

I picked up the newspaper and read the headline. A man and his wife were arrested this week in what police call a house burning scam! The article said they had moved ten times in ten years after their rental house burned to the ground. The family would have as many as half a dozen insurance policies on their possessions!

My heart sank like a stone in the creek when I read the family's name. I was the one who made the suggestion to give our graduation presents to this family. I was only able to contact a few of the other seniors and I offered to repay them for what they had given the family. Not one of them would accept my offer and they said, "It is not your fault. Do not worry about it. You did not make us do it; we did it on our own.

Another senior said, "Do not feel bad, we did something good and we were blessed for doing it."

The fancy mag wheels on my car now did not look so great. Every time I saw them I thought about how selfish I had been. Even though I had worked night and day for years to buy the car of my dreams in high school that was not good enough. I had to have fancy wheels, too. Maybe it was a little maturity and guilt that was beginning to set in.

I started attending college at night, so I could work full eight hour days. On the weekends I helped my parents on the farm and with their rental property. I tried to forget about the scam that had been pulled on me and the other graduates.

Then one Saturday morning as I returned to my car from a quick stop at a hardware store, I saw a teenage boy and girl standing beside my car.

As I approached, the teenage boy said, "I love those mag wheels.

The teenage girl smiled and said, "They are beautiful!"

The young couple was driving a Torino GT with the same kind of wheels my car had originally.

I asked the teenage boy, if he would like to swap his wheels for mine.

The young couple just stared at me like they were in shock. Finally, the girl responded, "Are you serious?"

I said, "I'm going to trade this car for a new one before long and it would trade just as well with your wheels on it as it would with these."

It only took about twenty minutes for the tire store across the street to change the wheels. The couple was still in shock when I paid the clerk and drove away.

As I looked back in my rear view mirror to take one last look at those fancy mag wheels now on the teenagers Torino, I thought, you know they are right. It does feel better to give than receive! I had just unloaded a fancy set of mag wheels, a footlocker full of guilt, and I made a couple of teenagers happy and it only took twenty minutes and twenty bucks! Not a bad deal at all!

Love and a Red Wagon

A mountain of sand has poured through the hourglass of time, but a special image has managed to stay on my mind for over forty years. The image of a tall slender woman probably in her fifties, but the deep lines in her face, told me that her life had been hard. The story in her eyes as well told me of hardship.

Her lightly graying hair was tied behind her head and laid gently on her shoulders. The simple print dress she wore told me she wasn't a complicated person and her plain cloth shoes probably covered her tired feet, but it was what she held in her right hand that touched a special nerve in my heart.

In her right hand she held the black metal handle of a red wagon, the kind that a small child would get for Christmas and jump for joy. In the red wagon was a small child, a pretty baby boy with a big smile and curly hair.

Day after day I would see this woman walking to and from the small town nearby and on her return trip she would be carrying a bag or box of something. I assumed this child was her grandchild, because of the age difference, but I knew this wasn't a case of a babysitter caring for a child, because of the gentle loving way she cared for this child.

She would pull the little red wagon along the dirt street next to a railroad track being careful to miss the bumps and when confronted by a barking dog she would quickly pick the child up and hug him till the dog walked away. If a car came by on a dry dusty day, she would once again pick the child up in her arms and turn her back to the dust to protect this little child.

I saw this lady, day after day and sometimes several times a day, as she traveled around this small little town with the little baby boy sitting in the red wagon being pulled along the way.

I knew that there must be another story about why this child was always with this loving woman, but I never had the nerve to ask. Sometimes I would pass them on my bike and wave and say hello. The tired looking frail woman always managed to smile and nod her head. I could tell that the smile on her face didn't come easily.

I wondered all these years about what the circumstances behind this woman and child were, and if the small child in the wagon ever realized how lucky he was. He's probably a married man now, living far away and has a family of his own. I wonder if he remembers riding in that little red wagon.

Most people that saw them together probably didn't see the important part of this picture. They would only see a woman and child and a red wagon, but I saw a love story that would pale Romeo and Juliet. When I look at the Mona Lisa all I see is a woman, but when I looked at this woman, I saw love in its purest form. A love like this can't be bought, sold, borrowed, or traded. It's not for rent and it can't be stolen like gold and riches, but a love pure and true, far out values all the wealth on earth.

In today's world there is so much greed. People trying to out achieve each other. There seems to be a contest to see who can buy the biggest house, drive the most expensive car, wear the most expensive clothes, join the most elite country clubs, but have lost sight of the most beautiful, wonderful, priceless things on earth. For that tired looking woman, baby boy, and a simple red wagon stood out as one of the most beautiful pictures of love I have ever seen.

Our Studebaker Truck

I was raised in the country on a farm in South Georgia. We raised timber, cattle, and produced turpentine. My dad also built houses, many of which he kept for rental property. We always had plenty of work to do and a day off was a rare event.

One of the fondest things we owned was an old Studebaker truck. My dad had bought it new before I was born. From the earliest memories of my life, I remember that faithful, but ugly truck. It had a blue cab, red wheels, and a hood ornament that looked like a battering ram. Well, even though it was ugly, it was one of the handiest things we owned. We hauled cars on it, lumber, fertilizer, turpentine, sand and other building materials, but the hauls I enjoyed the most was when my father and I made those long trips, over one hundred miles, to a paint plant in Brunswick.

When I heard that dad was going to make that trip, I would put on my jeans and shirt the night before instead of my pajamas. Then in the middle of the night, I would take the pillow off of my bed and lay it on the floor in front of the front door to our house. Then just before daylight, when dad tried to leave, he would take the hint and throw me over his shoulder and bring my pillow along. He would start up that old ton and a half flatbed Studebaker truck and I would go back to sleep as he drove toward Brunswick.

As the sun started to shine over the dash, I would wake up and stretch. I would ask my dad, "Were we there, yet?"

Of course dad's answer was, "Not yet, son."

My dad was a big guy, 6'4", over 285 pounds. I couldn't have had a better dad. I loved him and I knew he loved me. People used to call me his shadow, because I followed him around everywhere he went.

Now that old Studebaker did have one major flaw, it always ran hot on long trips, so on the trip to Brunswick we always left early, because we would have to stop in Baxley for it to cool off.

Dad thought the devil himself must have lived in the radiator of that old Studebaker truck. He had explained to everyone that it had overheated since it was new and no matter what he did it always overheated on trips of fifty miles or more.

We always stopped at a little service station and café in Baxley. Dad knew the people well and while the Studebaker boiled over, we enjoyed a great breakfast. The man and woman that ran the combination restaurant and service station always treated us like family. I once remarked that mom made me chocolate milk for breakfast at home and from then on the sweet young lady that ran the café side of the business always made me chocolate milk. After enjoying a good breakfast and letting the truck cool, dad and the man caught up on old news.

We would leave, but before we left the lady always kissed me on the face and dad shook hands with the man and it was back to the "Beast" as dad called it and away we would go.

When we finally arrived at the paint factory, dad would back the truck up to the loading dock as the truck hissed its objections, already overheating again. The men at the plant would load the truck with paint.

We owned over thirty wood-sided houses, so we had to buy paint almost every year, so we made the trip together. We walked into the office where the tall thin man always welcomed us with a big smile and a handshake for my dad and he always rubbed my head. I couldn't figure out when I was a kid why so many people rubbed my head. Later on I was told it was supposed to be good luck to rub a red-headed kid on the head. Well, at least he didn't try to kiss me like the lady at the restaurant.

After paying for the paint, we would walk about one quarter of a mile along the road to a place that made all sorts of seashell ornaments. Usually, half of the truck bed was free after the paint was loaded, so my dad bought two hundred sea shell nightlights.

Now a seashell nightlight was a seashell about the size of a football with a poured plaster base with a colored light bulb inside and an electrical wire run through a hole in back, so you could plug it into an electrical socket and the seashell would light up and throw colored shadows on the wall behind it.

My dad had a plan for everything. We could easily haul two hundred nightlights back. We paid one dollar each for them and could easily sell them for one dollar and fifty cents each and profit one hundred dollars that would pay for half of the paint.

As soon as the paint was loaded on the truck, we drove over to the loading dock down the street and loaded the two hundred nightlights. Then we would refill the now cool radiator and drive back to the little café and service station in Baxley which was half way home for us. We would eat fried chicken and biscuits while the "Beast", the truck, cooled down again.

I asked my dad why the Studebaker got so hot. He told me that it had run hot from the first day he had bought it. He said he had returned it to the dealer several times, but they couldn't find the problem.

Several years went by and my father gave the old Studebaker to one of my older brothers. My brother had the engine torn down and they found what was left of a mechanic's grease rag stuffed inside the return water port of the head. My father later found out that the mechanic at the dealership had sabotaged the truck. He was mad that dad had bought it instead of a potential customer he had been working on. He would have earned a twenty dollar bonus, if his customer had bought the truck.

When my father returned the truck to the dealer, the angry mechanic just lied and said he couldn't find the problem. My father was amazed he had no idea that had happened. He said he would have been glad to give the mechanic the twenty dollars, if he had known.

My father and I had made many trips in the old Studebaker truck from the time I was a toddler to the last time when I was fourteen, when I finally got to take the big steering wheel in my own hands. I only got to drive it a few feet, because the brakes had failed.

Years later, I dreamed about one of our earlier trips in the old Studebaker. Dad had stopped at our driveway and let me out! I was on the way to see him and tell him about my dream when I got the word that my father had died, but I had a feeling since he and I were so close that he might have had the same dream. I don't know if there are any Studebaker trucks in heaven, but I wish he and I could take another trip, just one more time, some day.

A Tragedy and a Miracle!

It was a rainy, cold afternoon as the yellow school bus turned around just south of the Dodge County line in Telfair County, Georgia. Mr. Dollar, the bus driver, his wife, and their grandbaby were the only remaining occupants of the bus as it lumbered back onto the highway and proceeded south.

Mrs. Dollar worked in the cafeteria at the McRae-Helena School and she rode to and from her job with her husband each day.

The Dollars lived on a small farm just down the road and were on their way home. The Dollars raised hogs on their small farm, but like most small farmers they had to have jobs to supplement their farm income. Their daughter who was married to a young soldier stationed in Texas had been staying with them since their baby was born. She had just acquired an afternoon job at a store in town and would drop off the baby at the lunch room around one o'clock each day on her way to work.

Mrs. Dollar was sitting in the seat directly behind her husband and held the three month old infant. She had wrapped the baby up in a blanket to keep him warm on such a cold, rainy afternoon.

Mr. Dollar slows the bus down to make a left hand turn, as a heavy rain pounds the top of the bus' roof, so loud, it's almost impossible for them to hear anything.

The narrow dirt road has a steep climb until it reaches the Southern Railroad tracks and then levels off on the other side only a few hundred feet from the old wooden gate that leads to their farm.

Mr. Dollar shifts the bus into double low gear and presses the accelerator to the floor in order to climb the steep hill that leads to the railroad tracks. Trees fill in the narrow strip between the highway and the railroad obscuring the view, as they sway back and forth in the wind blown rain.

A woman, just a few hundred yards north, walks out on her front porch to check on some plants hanging in baskets around the edge of her front porch.

Suddenly a lightning bolt strikes just south of her location. As she turns toward the flash of light, she sees the most horrible sight imaginable. She sees the front of a yellow school bus as it pulls onto the railroad tracks and the front of the locomotive with its big round light, a split second before the front of the school bus explodes into pieces.

She is so shocked she rubs her eyes and looks back again as she hears the thunder and the results of the horrible impact and sees pieces of the bus falling like debris from an explosion.

The front portion of the bus is instantly gone and the back of the bus spins around and lands at the bottom of the road, next to the highway.

The train's whistle and brakes scream as steam from what was the bus' radiator instantly encases the locomotive, like a cloud. As the locomotive's brakes lock, the bang, bang, bang, of the boxcars' hitches slamming into each other and the train's horn could be heard for several miles.

As the train finally came to a stop, the winds cease and the heavy rain is now just a drizzle. The sun begins to peek through the dark clouds as the reality of the tragedy sets in.

The train's engineer, who only saw the bus when the lightning flashed just before the impact, had grabbed the brake lever and strap for the whistle at the same time as hundreds of pieces of glass, steel, and wood peppered the locomotive.

The engineer was absolutely horrified as he desperately tried to stop the train. Engineers live with the fear of striking a vehicle at a crossing, but a bus load of kids is such a horrible thought that the engineer can barely comprehend the magnitude of what has just happened.

A truck stops along the highway and the driver is so shocked he has trouble remembering how to open the door.

Farmers, area residents, and travelers along the highway arrive on the scene as the engineer finally manages to stop the train several hundred yards up the track. The engineer is so shocked that he trips and falls as he tries to climb down from the cab of the big locomotive.

As people arrive on the scene, a desperate search is made for the passengers and the driver of the bus. A neighbor of the Dollar family explains that they were on their way home after dropping off all of the school children. A sigh of relief comes over the crowd as they are told no students would have been on the bus, but the stress returns when the neighbor explains that the driver, his wife, and their infant grandchild would have been on the bus.

It only takes a few minutes to find the badly mangled bodies of Mr. Dollar and his wife as the search continues for the body of the baby in the blood splattered debris.

The neighbor continues to explain that the Dollars' daughter and mother of the missing baby has a part-time job in town at about 1:00 p.m. She would drop the baby off at the school lunch room so her mother could look after the child for her and then bring the child home on the bus. The neighbor continues and says she gets off about 5:00 p.m. She will be coming home soon, so we need somebody to go to the store where she works and break the terrible news to her there, so she won't just drive up on this tragic scene. The neighbor had made this plea for help, because his car was blocked by the train on the other side of the track.

No one volunteers for the job as they all realize the magnitude of the situation. Just imagine how hard it would be to tell a young woman that she has lost her mother, father, and her baby.

A young state trooper arrives on the scene and parks his patrol car on the shoulder of the road. He has only been on the job a few days and is amazed at the tragedy he sees in front of him.

The people on the scene explain to the trooper that the two adult victims' bodies have been located, but the body of a baby that would have been with them has not been located.

A young minister and his wife arrive on the scene and after being informed of the situation, the minister asks the people to join him in prayer. All of the people gather around the minister and they get down on their knees. The minister prays for mercy and strength for the Dollar family and especially for the young mother who will soon be told that she has lost her parents and her child. The minister also prays for divine guidance in the search for the baby.

As the minister ends his prayer with Amen, the people rise and see a rainbow and the sun shines brightly.

The people resume their search. Suddenly everyone stops and looks around. They hear a baby crying in the distance. People were asking each other if they were traveling with a baby, but everyone says no. Then suddenly, someone yells, the crying is coming from that way and points toward the locomotive where it came to a stop up the tracks.

As the searchers run down the side of the boxcars toward the big locomotive, they have to be careful to avoid pieces of debris from the bus. The people reach the front of the locomotive. They find it is partially covered by part of the bus' roof. They work in unison to remove the debris from the train's large front bumper, better known as a cow catcher, and find a crying baby wrapped in a white blanket.

The minister picks up the baby and looks up to the sky and says, "Praise God!"

The crowd is absolutely amazed that the child appears to be unharmed. Instantly the crowd cheers as the minister climbs down the front of the train holding the child.

In all the joy of finding the baby, the mother needs to be told of the tragedy before she leaves work and drives up on the scene.

The trooper asks if anyone would like to accompany him to McRae to return the child to its mother and tell her the tragic news about her parents and about the miracle of the baby's survival!

The young minister and his wife agree to accompany him.

This combination of tragedy and miracle took place in Telfair County around 1937. My father told me this story in 1957 the night after we lost a neighbor and friend. Her name was Sara Coleman. I was only six years old at the time, but I still remember this beautiful, kind, considerate young woman. She was killed driving a brand new Chevrolet car on a winding dirt road only about ½ mile from our home. Her death was a tragic loss to us all. But just like the story about the Dollar family, Sara's two daughters, one just a toddler and the other one about eight years old, both survived without major injuries.

The Coleman families were salt-of-the-earth people and we were fortunate to have them as friends and neighbors.

Yellow Hammer

From days gone by, the home of my youth was a big, long, white house that sat on a hill across the highway from Coleman's Grocery and Rolling Store. Our house sat perpendicular to the highway and we had a big, circular driveway that circled right by the front porch. Our property was covered with trees, shrubs, and flowers. My Mom's green thumb was very apparent to travelers on US 341 Highway. A springtime photo of our place had more colors than a large box of crayons.

In our back yard sat a strange looking shiny aluminum tank that we utilized as a fuel oil tank. The story I was told was this big shiny round thing that was pointed on each end was a surplus fuel tank sold at auction from Robins Air Force Base. The tank lay on its side across a platform made out of four fence post and a couple of boards about five feet above the ground. The fuel oil would flow through a copper tubing down to the ground and come up right under the furnace in our home.

Every morning about sunrise a strange yellow bird would land on top of the shiny tank and start pecking on the tank. The Rata-Tata-ta-ta-ta noise was so loud that you could hear it a mile away. My bedroom was, unfortunately, the closes to the tank and some mornings I actually fell out of bed before I realized it was only our feathered visitor.

I had no idea what caused this bird to perform this early morning ritual, but when the power went off after a storm, it was very helpful.

The problem was, it came every morning, including Saturday, Sundays, and holidays. It never discriminated. It always woke us up. We had to warn overnight guest about our special alarm clock, so they wouldn't panic from the sudden sharp noise.

I often wondered, "Did this yellow bird mistake the shiny fuel tank for a large pecan or was it an extraterrestrial being trying to communicate with its home planet?"

Then one morning the visitor stopped just as suddenly as it had started. I had become so accustomed to the very noisy visits that I found myself waking up just after daylight and looking out the window for the elusive and talented little alarm clock with feathers.

Then the guilt sat in as I remembered all of the times I had opened the window and yelled, "Shut up!" at the yellow bird.

I actually missed the early wake up calls. Isn't it funny how you miss some things after they are gone, when you didn't particularly care for them before?

I began to realize that the yellow bird might have reached the end of his life span, or had a bad encounter with a predator of some sort, but of all things I actually missed its visits.

Our farm stretched over half a mile from our home in the direction of Jay Bird Springs. On the other end of our farm were a big barn and a pond.

My Dad had just built a little one bedroom cottage between the barn and the pond as sort of a little fun place to retreat on weekends. The cabin as we called it was now complete and we decided to spend the night in it to break it in. The only bedroom had bunk beds and I volunteered to sleep on top right next to a window.

As everybody else went to sleep and my Dad started snoring, I lay on my side staring out the window until I finally drifted off to sleep.

Sweet, beautiful sleep, after being awake so late, it felt good to escape to a place of temporary rest.

Then as the sun slowly rose over the little cabin, Rata-Tata-ta-ta-Tata!

I sat up suddenly and hit my head on the ceiling! I could not believe my ears. As I looked out the window to see, the little yellow hammer pecking the top of the 55 gallon metal barrel fuel tank directly below the window. I was happy to see the little yellow bird had not expired, but just change locations. Then it occurred to me to always appreciate the little things in life, because they can leave the biggest memories!

Turpentine Story

I was raised in the country just north of Helena, Georgia, in the Deep South. We lived on a farm where we raised cattle and timber. We also sold turpentine in the fall of the year. It was a good cash crop.

There was a crew of men that worked the trees and collected the pine tar in small tin cups about the size of a brick. They would rip the bark off of a pine tree near the bottom for about a foot long and a few inches wide, then nail on a tin strip that worked like a funnel and the tar ran down the strip of tin and into the cup.

Then the crews would collect the cups of tar and scrape the tar into large fifty-five gallon wooden barrels with metal bands around them. Usually it was late in the afternoon before dad had time to collect the barrels.

He would hook a four- wheel farm wagon behind our old Allis Chalmers tractor and drive through the woods to collect the tar barrels. As we loaded full barrels on the back of the wagon, we left empty barrels at each stop to be filled again and to be picked up on the next trip. The barrels full of tar were very heavy, so dad used a heavy oak plank that also doubled as a tail board on the wagon as a gang plank to roll the barrels up on the wagon.

When the wagon was full, we would tow it out to the bank along the highway where dad would park our ton and a half farm truck on one side and the wagon on the other. Then we would carefully roll the heavy barrels on the bed of the truck for shipment to the turpentine still.

Even though it was a lot of hard work, I enjoyed helping my dad on the farm.

After loading the barrels, the trip to the turpentine still was only a few miles. When we arrived at the plant, someone would come out of the office and count the barrels and give us a slip of paper as a receipt. Then we would gently drive up a ramp to a large square building where the barrels were rolled off of our truck onto a scolding hot steel floor that tapered to the middle to a round hole.

My father explained that a flame under the steel floor kept it hot so the tar in the barrels would melt and run down that hole in the center. They would then boil, filter, and screen the tar into a clear liquid product called turpentine.

Now turpentine was used in hundreds of ways. It was used in paints, cleaning products, and it even had medical uses for people and farm animals.

After the barrels were emptied, we would go up the steep ramp to retrieve our barrels.

My dad and I with our old Studebaker truck lumbered back home. Before we went into the house after parking the Studebaker truck, we made a trip to the barn to wash off any remaining pine tar from our hands, and of course to remove the tar, we had to use, you guessed it, turpentine.

I don't know anybody that collects pine tar for the turpentine anymore. I guess in today's world of high tech chemicals and the like maybe it's not needed anymore, but I have many fine memories of ridding through the woods on the seat beside my dad on that old Allis Chalmers tractor of ours hauling barrels of pine tar to our faithful old Studebaker truck. Maybe collecting turpentine has gone out of style, but those fine memories of a simpler time never will!

Fire

When I was a college student, in of all places, Cochran, Georgia, I lived in a little shack near a place called Frazier. Now I know a guy as dumb as me has about as much business going to college as a polar bear, but to please my mom, I gave it a shot. I actually did succeed at something that every Georgia Governor since Reconstruction had failed to achieve. I turned Middle Georgia College into a four year institution.

The lady next door utilized her house as a kind of daycare center. She took care of several kids, usually after lunch, about 1 o'clock, she and the kids would generally take a nap. However on this day, it became painfully aware to my bloodshot eyes that smoke was bellowing out of the eves of the house next door. Seeing her car in the driveway, I assumed she and the kids were taking an afternoon nap.

A chance like this only comes once in a lifetime. I ran to the house and grabbed the screen door locked tighter than the rack on a moose, so I just snatched it open with all my might and with five gallons of adrenalin to spare; the door was ripped right off its hinges. I felt like Superman. Next I just kicked the entrance door and it fell in flatter than a pancake. Boom! The smoke hit me like a hot black cloud. Then I had to think, (which is something I only do when I have to), and I remembered Fireman Freddie's lecture in the third grade. Probably the only thing I learned in the third grade. Get down on your hands and knees and crawl around and find those kids, you dummy.

Well I crawled and crawled trying to find those kids and the lady of the house. I turned over a table and chairs and ran into several walls and a magazine stand, but no kids could be found. By now I'm panicking. Needing some fresh air, I crawled back out of the house and ran next door to get the lady that lived next door to call the fire department.

Fortunately, before I choked to death in the house on my third or fourth search, the Fire Department arrived and went straight to work, breaking out the windows, chopping holes in the roof, and pouring hundreds of gallons of water on the fire.

"Find the kids! Find the kids!" I was shouting.

So several brave fire fighters raced into the house and moments later they returned with a badly burned pot roast. Apparently that was the source of the smoke.

I had ripped the screen door off the hinges, kicked in the door, and crawled around in a house full of smoke, raced next door, and had a neighbor call the fire department to rescue an over-cooked pot roast.

Standing there with egg on my face and soot to go with it, feeling like the village idiot and thinking, it couldn't get worse than this. Then the lady of the house arrived with a half dozen kids riding with another lady friend of hers and screamed, yelled, and hollered at me for destroying her furniture. The house was rented, but the furnishings including the pot roast, was hers.

Feeling lower than a wagon rut, I slithered back to my hut. Can you hear that music playing in the background from the Charlie Brown series when he felt like a failure?

A quick shower and off to work. For once, I was glad to get to work.

Later that night the owner of the house next door came by and chewed me out for destroying his house.

First thing the next morning, I heard a loud knock on my door. A fireman delivered a bill for calling a fire truck outside of the city limits.

You would think after an experience like this, my hero fire fighter days would be over, but less than a year later at a Jaycees convention in Atlanta in a very fancy and very dark restaurant, I hear a sudden "Plof" and a flash of light.

I instantly doused the fire at the table behind us with the pitcher of water from our table. Even in the dark, I could see an angry, wet man, woman, and chef holding two shish-ka-bobs still smoldering! Needless to say, I didn't stay for dessert.

So there are heroes and zeroes. As for me, I wouldn't report a fire again, unless I was held at gun point by Smokey the Bear himself.

The Race

It was a beautiful fall night. I had just left my evening class at Middle Georgia College in Cochran, Georgia. After putting in eight hours of work and racing forty miles to my night classes and two hours of the most boring lectures on earth, I had finally been set free.

My red Road Runner was shining like new again with its two fresh coats of wax applied just days before as I turned in at the Brazier, the official hangout for young folks in those days. There right in front of me was my girlfriend and her cousin, Elroy. I couldn't think of two people I'd rather see. As I pulled up beside them, I hit the power windows button for the passenger side and invited them to join me. What a relief! I felt 100% better. As we laughed and talked, an old white 57 Chevy slowly rolled around the Brazier. The engine was real rough sounding. It must have had a race cam!.

Elroy spoke up and said "Wow"! That must be the Hot-Rod I've heard so much about."

Apparently two brothers that owned a local auto parts store had been building this car over a period of several years.

"Every available Hot-rod part from here to California had been acquired to make this the fastest Hot Rod on the east coast," he explained.

"Yes," I said, "I've heard about it myself."

Apparently it would be a good advertisement for their auto parts business.

Several times the white 57 Chevy came around the circular drive with its large rear drag slick tires, traction bars, plainly visible. The radical sound of its engine on occasion revved up to show they meant business. Every time it stopped in front of us, he gunned his engine and pointed at his hood. This was a well-known gesture. He was challenging me to a race.

No way, I waved him off each time. I was trying to relax and enjoy my friends company after a long hard day. Besides my car was stock. No race cam or dragster tires or drag bars, just stock. Now my car was no wimp either. It had a 383 cubic inch engine with over 300 hp, but it should be no match for this Race-Rod Hand Built speed monster we had heard so much about.

After challenging several other guys with no takers, the Bad Boy 57 Chevy pulled up beside my Road Runner on the driver's side.

The driver actually reached out and tapped the window of my car and yelled, "Is that a Road Runner or is that a Chicken?"

Then he and his passengers laughed profusely.

Instantly the engine in my car roared to life. The transmission jumped into drive and I had to use both feet on the brakes to keep it from running over the building ahead. The last thing I wanted that night was a hair-raising, blood-boiling, drag race especially against a Hot Rod, but when you call somebody's Road Runner a Chicken; It's worse than a dare; It's worse than a double dare. It borders challenging patriotism, mother, apple pie, baseball, and the American way of life.

"Where?" I asked loudly.

The location was agreed on. Elroy hustled my girlfriend, his cousin, out of the vehicle so that she could take her car safely home. We had business to handle.

As the 57 Chevy and my Road Runner left the Brazier, the tires were screaming. A dozen or so young people followed us as we roared toward the well-known road just outside of town where drag race challenges were usually settled. Was I nuts? Here I was about to race a car professionally prepared over a period of years to be a drag race monster against my stock 1969 Plymouth Road Runner muscle car. Sure my car was fast and would run the numbers off the speedometer top end racing, but drag racing. What had I gotten myself into? My car was fancy, but an automatic, what was I thinking? We arrived at the location. The others, mostly teenagers parked along the sides of the road waiting for the show. Two guys in a Mustang drove down to the other end of the plainly marked ¼ mile, ready to signal when clear.

Elroy looks over at me. "Are we crazy?" He asked. "We can't possibly outrun this professionally built race car with a stock Road Runner."

The driver of the 57 Chevy looks over and yells, "$50.00 and a case of beer."

"Alright," we motioned. "Yes, thumbs up."

Now we're in real trouble. Between us, we don't have $50.00 or any beer, but by this time, the red paint on my car, my red hair and my face were all the same color.

Just a week before a great mechanic in Warner Robins had tuned up my car. He was a Mopar fanatic and as I was leaving his shop, he said, "By the way, I set up your car for drag racing, just drop it in Drive and gently mash the throttle to the floor."

Why had he told me that? I had never drag raced it before.

The headlight of the spotter's car flashed. That meant the road was clear for miles and another guy flagged us by dropping his arms. I had to fight temptation to just floor my car, but I remembered what my mechanic had told me.

"If you drag race it, just leave the automatic shifter in Drive and gently mash the accelerator to the floor. If you stomp it, you'll lose traction," He remarked.

Heck! Then and there, I remembered of all people, a preacher had taught me to drag race. Can you believe that? He had explained, "Don't spin your wheels, you'll just loose traction. Let the other guy be the show-off and you'll win every time."

As the signal came, I fought the urge to stomp the accelerator through the floor. Five gallons of adrenalin flowed through my body. Even though it was a chilly night, sweat was pouring down my face. As I gently pressed the accelerator to the floor, my car surged forward, barely barking the tires. My four barrel carburetor moaned. I glanced over to my right at the 57 Chevy. I had left him in the smoke from the tires of his own car.

As my car speedometer jumped forward, changed into second again, barking the tires for just a second. I looked in my rear view mirror to see the 57 Chevy shrinking smaller and smaller as my Road Runner crossed the Finish line like a bullet.

The guys at the Finish line and about 30 or so spectators along the way were cheering. It took a pretty good distance to bring my car to a full stop from over 100 mph.

Where was the 57 Chevy? It finally came by, but it didn't stop. We didn't get the $50.00 or the case of beer. But I got more satisfaction and excitement out of that race than money could ever buy.

No one ever saw the 57 Chevy again. Rumors were they burned the car out of anger. Some rumors that the owners shot the car all to pieces. Still others claim the owners shot the car to pieces and burned it. I guess they should have thought twice before calling my Road Runner a "Chicken."

The next day I went to thank the mechanic for the advice he had given, only to find out that he had died at about the exact time I was involved in the race.

He was a fine man and a fine mechanic. I still miss him. I wanted so badly to tell him about the race, but somehow I had the feeling he might have been watching over us that night from above. How else could my stock production car have blown the doors off a monster street rod!

The Cake

In the fall of 1976 on the 200th anniversary of our Great Nation, I was busy building houses in Houston County, Georgia. I sold one to an older couple that proved to be a challenge to please! This older couple now might have looked frail and helpless, but looks are deceiving. The old man was grouchy as an old bear with diaper rash, but the little old lady could have probably come out on top in a couple of rounds with Hulk Hogan.

I rode by their house one Saturday morning and noticed the heating and cooling contractor's van sitting out front. Worried about the safety of the contractor, I stopped and rang the doorbell. Ding Dong!

Suddenly this old lady appeared at the door carrying a long barrel 38 pistol from the early twenties.

"What's wrong Ma'am?" I asked.

She shrieked, "That no-good SOB came by to check my dehumidifier and spilled that pink stuff on the floor in the hall. When he comes down, I'm going to shoot him."

I did my best to calm her down. In the process, I would try to help the poor, sweated down hostage in the attic, to escape. Then I complimented her furnishings and curtains in a way that Eddie Haskell would have been impressed.

A few days later I rode by their house again and noticed a very anxious power company meter reader frozen like a pretzel in the corner of her yard near the electrical meter. What had started so innocently as a simple reading of the meter had become a stand-off at the OK Corral. This time she had this poor guy cornered with her kitchen knife. Again I intervened and explained that this guy wasn't a pervert or "peeping Tom," just an employee of the power company. This guy still turns pale, if anyone mentions this little altercation.

One Friday morning as I turned the corner in front of her house, there she stood waving for me to stop. I remember looking for the old long barrel 38 or her butcher knife!

After stopping, I noticed her hand gesturing for me to follow her.

We entered the garage where she explained that the stove door on her new oven would burn her hand after baking for only a few minutes. As she continued to down-rate the supposedly poorly insulated stove door, I was somewhat relieved. So far, she had complained about everything from the foundation to roof and now it was the stove door that had her upset.

I quickly removed the oven door, apologized for the problem, and told her I would return in plenty of time for her to fix supper and quickly drove away. I had planned to return to my warehouse and exchange the oven door and retrieve another one, trying once again to please this cranky old lady.

Several hours passed as I ran here and there trying to keep the sub-contractors supplied, when I suddenly realized I had forgotten to exchange the door. By now the warehouse would be locked up tighter than a walnut shell.

What was I going to do? Then that defective little brain of mine came up with an idea. I stopped my pick-up and opened the tool box and retrieved my handy spray bottle of glass cleaner. In just a few minutes; the oven door looked shiny as new again. Even the factory stickers were still on the door. I returned the door to granny, the bone-crushers' house, and I apologized for being late. I placed the door on the oven and hastily made my retreat to the open door of my faithful Ford and away I escaped! Now how did I get myself in this mess? Now I know how Butch Cassidy and the Sundance Kid must have felt when they took off to Bolivia.

Monday morning I turned the corner and there she stood at the end of her driveway wearing a housecoat and combat boots. OK, so I lied about the combat boots, but anyway. I was absolutely terrified. I couldn't believe it. Was she actually smiling or was I hallucinating? Now I'm really scared. Where's my gun? Was she packing heat? Why didn't I join the Marine Corp like my friend, Elroy? Then I would be one of the few good men! My spine turned to jello. My knees were knocking so bad I could barely focus my eyes. Why did I stop? I could have easily run down this old gal and swore it was an accident. Heck, I could have blamed it on the sun shining in my eyes. I might have even managed a couple of tears. If nothing else I could have thought about the damage to my new pick-up. No, I had already stopped. What an idiotic thing to do? Why am I so scared of this Granny Clampett look alike? It is a smile. I guess she hadn't used it very often. Be brave, you coward. Where's my gun! I know it's in here somewhere. Oh, well it's too late.

"Good morning, honey," she said.

Now I know I'm going to die a cruel and bloody end to such a wonderful guy!

"I just wanted to thank you for trading that stove door for me. The other one would burn my hand if I touched it after only a few minutes of baking, but this new one was still so cool I could lay my hand on it after baking all afternoon."

Then I noticed a box in her hands. Was it full of dynamite or plastic explosives or maybe a hand grenade? Opening the box, I cringed and braced for the worst. What? A cake! What was this old bat doing standing out on her driveway, seven-thirty in the morning in her housecoat with a cake!

"I baked this one just for you, Hon!" she said.

Imagine being called "Hon" by Mrs. Frankenstein.

As I regained enough energy to reach out the window and accept the cake from her, I said, "Thank you, Ma'am. I am so touched by your act of kindness that I don't know what to say."

So I quickly excused myself and drove away. Can you believe this? Who knows, that old gal might not be so bad after all, but there's no way I'm going to find out the hard way by trying to eat this strange cake. I drove to one of my construction sites at the other end of the street. I stopped

114

and pitched the cake out of the window to some stray dogs. Their tails were wagging excitedly as they jumped in to gobble up the cake. You know, I never saw those dogs again. I guess I'll have it on my conscious forever that I threw that cake out the window rather than calling a hazardous waste management team.

"I'm sorry dogs. Please forgive me."

Strange New Home

It was a beautiful fall day in September 1990. I was on my way to deliver a tractor and mower just north of Athens, Georgia, after a right here and left there. I arrived at what I assumed was the meeting place for the delivery. I stopped at a gate on my left, just past a small country store that had been abandoned for forty years or more. An old rusty gas pump with a glass jar, and a rotten rubber hose protruded through the head high weeds.

This had to be the place. 5553 on the gate told me, yes, I was here. I looked around. Just beyond the gate, I saw a carport shelter and two Volvo's, one four door and the other was a wagon, this and the fact that I was near the University of Georgia told me that two college professors lived here.

The purchasers had not been to my sales lot. We had just made the deal over the phone, but where were they? The only other thing in sight was a strange looking greenhouse, just a hundred feet or so up the hill.

I parked in front of the gate and waited patiently for someone to show up. I found myself enjoying the scenery, and then as if from nowhere, a man and woman appeared at the gate.

I wondered, "Where did they come from?"

The couple was probably in their late fifties, both tall, graying hair, dressed in jeans and University of Georgia sweatshirts. The man had a big gold ring in his ear and a long pony tail. The woman had her hair cut very short. Both wore western boots. I thought they should have traded hair styles, but that was my opinion!

I stepped out of my rollback delivery truck and was greeted with smiles and hellos. I couldn't figure out how they had appeared so suddenly, but I figured it didn't matter.

I proceeded to show them the tractor still on the truck, because we had made a deal over the phone and had never met each other in person. Another happy customer in the area had referred us to them. It's always a good feeling to have other happy customers referring new customers to you. It makes you feel like you're doing a good job.

I unloaded the equipment and showed the new owners how to safely operate the tractor and mower. I even went into detail about how to maintain the service to keep it running good.

We completed the paperwork and I was ready to go when they asked me if I wanted to see their new home. I have found that when you sell equipment and deliver it to customers with a new home they like to show it off, so I agreed.

I asked them how far away it was, because I wanted to get back through Athens before 5:00 p.m. and the traffic jam hour.

They both laughed and said, "You're standing on top of it."

I looked around. I was in between the gate and the strange looking greenhouse.

They just pointed straight down, grinned, and said, "It's underground."

I must have seen everything on my deliveries, but a house underground. I have seen houses partially underground and some that were built by cutting into a hillside, but this one was a new one.

They led me down toward a strange looking greenhouse. The walls were glass and I saw copper tubing running up and down the wall and roof. They explained that was the source of hot water and additional heat; also there were mirrors that reflected light down two large open holes. They explained the mirrors provided light down below. She explained that she was a geophysicist and that her husband was an engineer, and that they had decided to build something different.

Now I realized how they had appeared so quickly. It was only about 100 feet from the gate to the strange greenhouse. There were steps and more steps as we wound our way down into what was apparently their home. It really was interesting how they had built it. The walls, floor, and ceiling were concrete.

The lady explained, "We wanted something different and we wanted something energy efficient and completely safe."

I looked around. There was a round upside down funnel looking metal fireplace near the center. Now I realized what the round looking pipe was for that also protruded up through the greenhouse. I must admit I was impressed.

The lady spoke, "This is a 100% safe home. Even though it's underground, it's high up on a hill. We are completely safe from floods, tornadoes, hurricanes, lightning, fire, hail. Absolutely, completely, safe," she said.

The man spoke, "It took us years to design it and build it, but it is worth it."

There is absolutely no peril on Earth that could hurt us." said the lady.

As I looked around, I must admit I was really impressed, but as usual, my brain got me in trouble. I spoke without thinking, I'm good at that. "What about earthquakes?"

Before the words were completely out of my mouth, I realized I shouldn't have said them.

The man looked at the woman, as she stared holes through the man, but total silence fell over them both.

I figured since I already had my check and the tractor and equipment had been unloaded from my truck, it just might be a good idea to leave. I walked quietly toward the winding stairs. I looked back to take one last look at the man and woman, still standing staring at each other.

Then, I quickly walked up the stairs and exited the underground fortress.

I can still remember the couple staring at each other. I guess earthquakes hadn't occurred to them.

The Fifty Years Are Up

In days gone by, I was a country boy from South Georgia. My parents, three older brothers, a sister, and I lived in a big white house on our farm just north of McRae, Georgia. A little country store on the other side of the road was our only visible neighbor, other than the travelers on U.S. 341, a major highway through our state.

It was April 1 and just about dark when one of my older brothers came home. This brother was just as cool and calm as he entered the living room and as he walked through going to his bedroom to change clothes, he very calmly remarked, "The store's on fire."

I was watching television and my Mom had set up her ironing board in the living room to keep me company. Now this particular brother was the one that enjoyed a good prank and could tell some of the tallest tales on earth. He could confound the best bull skipping gurus, fortunetellers, or psychiatrist on earth.

My Mom dropped her iron and said, "That's it! I'm tired of your tricks and stories."

She marched around the corner directly behind my brother as she gave him a good tongue lashing for telling stories. My brother continued to change his shirt without saying a word or breaking his cool, calm composure. My Mom was pointing her finger at him, as she continued to give him a big tongue lashing.

I turned and looked out the triple set of windows in our living room to see the biggest fireball I had ever seen in my short life. I couldn't believe it! The flames were reaching up into the surrounding trees. It looked like the whole world to the north of us was in flames. I ran to where my mother was still giving my brother a "finally had enough tongue lashing and started yelling, "Mom, Mom, Mom."

She didn't pay me any attention at all and my brother still as cool as could be, buttoned up his fresh shirt and was combing his hair getting ready for his date.

I tried and tried to get her attention as I looked back at the enormous fire, but she wouldn't be distracted from her attempt to correct my older brother. I finally had to grab her left hand and pull her out of the door way to my brother's room and screamed at the top of my lungs before I finally got my Mom's attention.

When she finally saw the fire, her expression was one of complete shock. Then she yelled, "The store is on fire, the store is on fire, the store is on fire!"

My brother just calmly walked by my Mom, who I was afraid was in shock and calmly said, "I tried to tell you."

As my brother walked out the front door, my mother just looked at the fire and said, "I can't believe it. He told the truth!"

We walked out the front door as my brother drove away to see cars parked along the highway as far as you could see. I guess they were watching the spectacular sight. It was cheap entertainment and more exciting than the July Fourth sparklers.

My Mom continued to hold my hand and mumble, "I can't believe it; he told the truth."

We sat down on the steps that led to a small front porch and Mom and I continued to gaze at the fire. I couldn't tell if my Mom was more shocked by the fire or the fact that my brother's tall tale was true.

My father didn't get home until after midnight. He had gone to Brunswick to get a truck load of paint. We had so many old rental houses that my Dad would buy paint by the truckload from the factory. When he came home, he didn't notice the old store building was gone. He had just sold the building to a man from town and he was going to move it to his farm to use for a barn. My Dad had sold him the old store building, because he wanted to build a larger one and, because it was under attack from termites.

The man who bought the building told my Dad he knew how to get rid of the pesky termites and had paid him in cash.

My father, after coming home so late, just quietly went to bed and didn't get the news till the next morning. After making the long trip to Brunswick in an old ton and half Studebaker truck, my father had slept late while Mom prepared breakfast. When my Dad finally arrived at the breakfast table, he sat down and picked up a cup of coffee and took a sip. Then my Mom told him that Jerome had walked in the house the night before and told her that the store was on fire.

My father laughed and said, "Well, you know better than to believe one of his stories!"

Then I said, "Dad, the store was on fire!"

Dad just grinned and took another sip of coffee. Then suddenly he noticed the serious look on my Mom's face, sat the coffee down, stood up and looked through the window toward the highway. My father couldn't have been more shocked if he had seen a ghost. My father yelled, "The store's gone?" and then he ran for the front door. I followed close behind.

When we arrived at what was a store building, but was now a pile of ashes, my father just shook his head and said, "He told the truth!"

Dad then looked back at me and said, "I thought they moved it while I was gone."

Then Dad looked back across the road toward our home and mumbled, "Well, the man paid me in cash and I bought the paint, but I wonder what he will say about this?"

As we stood there staring at the ashes, we heard the birds chirping in the trees behind what used to be the store. My father looked up and yelled, "Oh no! The fire killed my trees!"

My Dad was right; the fire had killed several large trees that provided shade for the store. He looked distraught about losing the trees, because he had planned to build a new store building on this exact site as soon as the old building was moved.

I tried to think of something to make my Dad feel better. I looked up at my Dad and said, "Well, at least it killed the termites!"

My Dad laughed and picked me up and put me on his shoulders and said, "You're right, son. They won't bother anybody else."

As my Dad turned and walked away with me on his shoulders, I heard him mumble, "And Jerome told the truth!"

As my father walked back toward our home, I looked back at what used to be a store. Mr. Shiverman and his wife had rented the store from my Dad since before I was born, but when his wife died, he had moved away. That was when my Dad discovered the termites and decided to sell the building to be moved and build a larger one.

I could still remember the store had a big round glass barrel full of penny wheel lemon cookies and the small red drinks my father would bring home for me. I could hear the Southern Railroad train blowing its whistle at Achord junction just south of us, as we crossed U. S. 341 on the way home. I wondered if the train's engineer would notice the old store was gone.

A few weeks later, my father had the lot cleared and had a new foundation laid for the new building. One day a man stopped at our house and told my Dad that the man that bought the building had no intention of moving it. He told us he simply gave my Dad one thousand dollars for the building, insured it for two thousand dollars and hired a shady character to burn it where it sat.

My father just looked at the man and said, "You can't be serious?"

The man replied, "As serious as a lightning strike!"

My father just shook his head in disbelief and said, "So that's why the buyer wasn't upset!"

As the man drove away, I asked my father, "Wouldn't that be against the law?"

My father just looked at me and said, "Son, this country is a little bit crooked from the Courthouse to the White House and please don't tell anybody this story for at least 50 years!"

The fifty years are up, Dad!!

The Train at Jay Bird

I was raised on a farm in South Georgia about a half mile west of a railroad stop called Achord, but we lived only about two miles as the wind blows from Jay Bird Springs. Now Jay Bird Springs had been in business since long before I was born. It had mineral water flowing wells, a bowling alley, skating rink, Olympic size swimming pools and last, but certainly not least, a miniature train.

Now at the time, Jay Bird Springs was owned by the Bland family, some of the best folks you would ever want to meet. This was the equivalent today of Six Flags or Disney World. When I went to visit my Mother's family, most of which lived near Macon, I couldn't help but brag about the fact that I lived near Jay Bird. This place was a family recreational area for the whole family.

The part I liked the most was the train. I fell so many times trying to learn how to skate that the manager of the skating rink gave me double my money back to leave. He was right. He probably saved my life. I wasn't much of a swimmer and my bowling wasn't going to get me a spot on the National Tour, but that train, that beautiful miniature train. I loved that train.

The train tracks wondered around behind the family picnic area and circled out into the woods over a stream, through a covered bridge and back through the woods, and then stopped at the station for more passengers.

I loved that train. It apparently had been made in Switzerland and used to haul coal out of a mine and I think it ran on diesel instead of steam, but that didn't matter to me. Every time I got near a dime, I would tell my parents I was going for a bike ride and wind up at the train's boarding area.

If the crowd was small, Mr. Evans, one of the nicest people on Earth, would let me ride until I got tired. Sometimes I would ride for an hour. I guess after that long I felt guilty and got off, but I never really got tired of that train.

When I was a kid in school we had Jay Bird Day, usually it was in the spring and different schools would come on different days. When our school came, I spent most of my day riding the train.

When I became a teenager, I would bring my dates there for a ride on the train. Even if I had to rent some kids to have an excuse to ride the train, I would. The bad thing about getting grown up is you can't have as much fun. If a thirty year old builds a tree house or makes a nice swing under a big oak tree, people would think you're crazy.

As the years went by, we moved away. I went to college and started a business in Warner Robins, then I got married and we had a daughter. This was my chance to go for train rides without people thinking I was ready for the basket weavers.

My plans were cut short when I found out that Jay Bird's had been sold and turned into some kind of private club. I was so disappointed. I held my breath until I turned blue, but nobody cared.

I would lay in bed at night and dream of riding that train. I bought a box of cereal once, because it had a picture of a miniature train on it. The cereal tasted like shredded cardboard, but the train was beautiful.

On a beautiful spring morning in April I received a call from an old friend of mine asking me if I was going to the Jay Bird Springs auction. I couldn't believe my ears. The new owners were going to sell the place, piece by piece, and the train and tracks were on the list. I raced to the door, because according to my friend the sale would start in about 30 minutes and I lived an hour or more away.

I jumped in my Ford Explorer pickup and hit the road. I drove like a stock car driver. I passed more cars than a log truck.

Everywhere I turned something held me up. Road construction was everywhere. The third time I came up on a road construction project, the southbound lane was moving. Great luck, I thought. The flagman had other plans. He tried to stop me from following the others in front of me, but I hit the accelerator and attempted to follow them anyway. The flagman was furious. He stepped in front of my pickup and hit the hood of my Ford pickup.

"Where in the heck do you think you are going? Didn't you see me with this stop sign and flag?" he screamed.

I was mad as heck. I stomped the parking brake to the floor and jumped out with my pad and pen. "What in the heck is your name, buddy? You better have a good reason for stopping me!" I screamed.

The flagman's complexion changed instantly. He dropped his flag and stop sign and said, "I'm sorry, I didn't know." Then he waved for me to go ahead.

I jumped back in my Explorer and smoked the fires as I took off. I had to. Time was running out.

I was only about a mile from the turn-off on 341 Highway that led to Jay Bird Springs. I hoped there wouldn't me much traffic on the road, because for the next three miles I planned to let it roll!

I hadn't given much thought to what in the heck I was going to do with the train and 1/3rd mile of track, but first I had to buy it. Then I could take the time to actually think.

I topped the hill and the noon freight train was crossing the tracks, blocking the road to Jay Bird. I couldn't believe it a big train might hold me up until I lost the chance to buy the little train of my dreams. Finally, the big train lumbered on by and the crossing arms lifted.

Now it was show-time. Nothing was going to stop me now!

The temperature outside was approaching ninety degrees and the sun was brighter than a bonfire as I stepped on the throttle. There was a small green Chevrolet parked on the shoulder of the road. The front tire was flat as a checker board and standing beside it was a frail little grey haired lady holding a small child in her arms.

130

I've got to stop. I've never left a woman with a flat tire stranded on such a hot day. I've got to stop, but if I stop, I might miss buying the train.

Then I heard a voice saying, "Forget her. Buy the train."

Then I heard another voice saying, "You can't leave them stranded like that on such a hot day!"

I stopped. Why do I have to always be Sir Lancelot? I turned around and parked behind the green Chevrolet. This will be the fastest tire change in the history of mankind, I thought.

I set the parking brake and flipped on the four-way flashers and jumped out of my Explorer.

"Do you have a spare and jack?" I yelled.

"Yes, right there in the trunk." She said.

"I'm in a real hurry so I need to work fast." I yelled.

I looked in the car and the keys were in the switch. I raced to the rear of the car and opened the trunk. What? Two saddles and about ten cases of beer were piled up right to the trunk lid. No time to waste. I threw the saddle on the ground behind the car along with a couple of blankets. Heck, these saddles were so big and heavy. She must have a couple of Clydesdales.

I stacked case after case of beer, and then there were tool boxes and enough junk to fill up two large dumpsters.

Finally, I got the spare tire. I spun the locking handle off faster than the spinners on a 56 Oldsmobile. I grabbed the spare tire and jack and raced to the front. I raced back to the trunk for the lug wrench. I couldn't find it anywhere.

"Do you know where the lug wrench is?" I asked.

What does it look like was the old lady's reply.

When a woman asks you what something looks like, forget it, you're toast.

I raced back to my pickup. My Ford lug wrench wouldn't fit her Chevrolet, but I had a cross lug wrench in my toolbox behind the cab. It would fit any brand auto. As usual, it was on the bottom. I just threw a bunch of my tools in the back of my pickup to get to the cross lug wrench.

Then I raced like a rabbit back to the front left wheel of her car. I had to loosen the lug nuts before I could jack up the car, otherwise I would have to hold the tire and turn the lug nuts. I broke the lug nuts loose in fifteen seconds flat, a Nascar official would have been proud. Then I started to jack up the car, but my cross lug wrench wouldn't work in her jack. I wouldn't think of asking her again about her lug wrench.

I just raced back to my toolbox and retrieved a large screw driver and then raced to the front of her car. I started working the lever on the jack up and down until the car started rising up off the ground. I should be through in 90 seconds at this rate I thought, but no, the car started rolling back. I had forgot, in my haste, to set the parking brake, so I let the car down and jumped inside her car and pressed the parking brake, but it didn't hold.

What in the heck am I going to keep the car from rolling while I change the tire? What could I put under the rear wheels?

I know, maybe Grandma.

No, I couldn't do that, so I raced back to the pickup trying to find something in a hurry to prop against the rear wheel. Bingo! A brick, just what I needed. I was supposed to go to the brick plant in Macon the next morning and match it up so I could finish work on a remodeling job I had going. The brick worked perfectly and I had the tire mounted in sixty seconds flat. It only took two minutes to unload the trunk, but it took four minutes to reload it. It was like something packaged in China. You can never put something packaged in China back in the box. I just threw it all in and said "to heck with it."

It took ten tries to get the trunk lid of the green Chevrolet to close when I realized that I had forgotten to put the flat tire in first. I just opened the back door and threw it in the back seat. She could let some of her men-folk put it back in the trunk later!

The lady opened her purse and offered me fifty cents for changing her tire. I wouldn't have done it for five thousand dollars in the hurry I was in.

So, I thanked the lady anyway and jumped back in my Explorer and smoked the tires in reverse to get away from the Chevrolet, so that I could make a wild and fast spinning U-turn.

I finally reached the auction. Dang! What a crowd. Nowhere to park, so I just stopped my Ford pickup in the middle of the street and locked down the parking brakes and exited like I was on fire.

"Sold!" the auctioneer shouted.

I ran up to a man and asked him, "What did they just sell?"

"The train." He said.

I couldn't believe it. If only I had left the old lady and baby beside the road, I could have bought the object of my temporary insanity.

I had left my pickup sitting in the road with the headlights on and the flashers flashing. I walked back to my pickup and pulled away from the crowd of people. I drove home feeling lower than a gum wrapper at the bottom of a storm drain.

When I drove up to my business, I realized I had to get my mind back on my business and maybe I wouldn't venture down the road toward Jay Bird for a while. That's it. I was going to pout for a while and not bless the people in the area with my presence for some time.

I parked my faithful Ford Explorer out front of my business and walked inside like nothing ever happened. I sat down at my desk and I thought I wouldn't go back down that way any time soon, even if the president of the United States of America begged me.

Then I saw a memo note on my desk. I picked up the note that said, "Don't forget to take the white brick in the back of your pickup to Macon first thing tomorrow morning to be able to match it up with the samples for the Anderson job."

The brick! I left the brick propped under the tire of the older lady's Chevrolet when I changed her tire!

I wondered, do normal people have days like this?

House Mover

I was in a big hurry recently to pick up some parts at Brooks Auto Parts in Warner Robins when one of many traffic lights brought my hurry to a halt. As I sat in traffic, I realized that every vehicle ahead of me had an out-of-state tag. Then it happened. My little shot-glass brain zoomed back over fifty years to a story that everybody in Middle Georgia should know.

In the early to mid-1950's there was talk about closing the base. The new jet planes needed longer runways. Unfortunately, Robins had brand new aircraft hangers at one end of the runways and a swamp and river at the other end.

Carl Vinson was a US Congressman at the time and he was head of the Armed Services Committee making every effort to save Robins. The bids to destroy the new hangers and rebuild new ones were several millions of dollars.

A Macon, Georgia man came forward and said he could move the hangers for a fraction of the cost.

The government's response was to send a group of engineers to study the possibility of moving these extremely large hangers. The study committee concluded that it was absolutely impossible to relocate the hangers, and then the talk returned about shutting down Robins.

Time was also a factor. It was estimated that it would take up to two years to tear down the hangers and build new ones. So time and money was working against the future of Robins Air Force Base.

The Macon man had a meeting with Congressman Vinson to discuss the committee's findings. The Macon man told Congressman Vinson that anything man-made could be moved with enough men, money, and equipment.

Seeing the determination in his eyes, Mr. Vinson over-ruled the Army Corp of Engineers and allowed the Macon man a chance to see if he could get one moved in ninety days. However, if for any reason, he failed, he would get nothing for his efforts.

The Macon man knew, if he failed, he would be financially destroyed for life, but he also knew how important Robins Air Force Base would be to the Middle Georgia area. The Macon man went to Atlanta and bought on credit several large trucks, hydraulic jacks, and all the steel beams and wood pilings he could find.

The next day he hired every man he could find, even picking up hitch-hikers along the way. The crews worked around the clock. Tents were erected and filled with folding cots so the workmen could keep the project going. Finally, just over a month later, the first hanger was loaded and ready to go. A total of sixteen semi-trucks and trailers, four under each corner, all pulling in unison couldn't budge the giant structure.

The base commander and one of the young airmen jumped in a jeep and drove down the runway and in a few minutes they returned driving two very large bulldozers.

137

The dozers were chained, one to each corner of the hanger, and chains were run from the lead trucks to the rear trucks.

After the big dozers were connected, the man from Macon motioned with his arms for the dozers to tighten up the chains. Then, he motioned for the sixteen truck drivers to follow and the hanger began to rise up out of the ground and there was no turning back.

Within a matter of a few hours, the hanger was ready to be unloaded at its new location. Within ninety days, all of the hangers were moved and were being secured in their new locations.

The move project was a complete success and the man from Macon was told by Congressman Carl Vinson to submit his bill. Up to this point, the man from Macon had begged, borrowed and charged everything. He had saved the government nearly twenty million dollars and completed the project in just over four months.

The Army Corp of Engineers said it would take two-three years and twenty plus million dollars, but more importantly, he had saved Robins Air Force Base for the people of Middle Georgia.

The man from Macon presented his bill for $1.2 million dollars. This man had risked his entire financial future. If this project had failed, he would have been totally destroyed. This man knew how important the Base would be for our future, furthermore think about the fine people the Base has drawn like a magnet from all across the United States.

Our daughter met her husband at Robins. He was born in California. Now just imagine the thousands of couples who wouldn't be married to each other and the thousands of children these couples had. Then before you get through, figure how much money Middle Georgia would have lost, if the Base had been closed in the early mid-1950's!

All of this was possible, because a Middle Georgia Congressman had a good friend who had a truck load of confidence, common sense, enthusiasm, insight, and the guts to take a chance and save the Base. This man's name was Willis Jackson Watson.

After saving the Base, he went on to become one of the best house movers and building wreckers on the east coast. He moved buildings for the state that no one else would touch. He moved two, and in a few cases, three story brick mansions when the interstate come through Macon that people said couldn't be moved.

Mr. Watson had a motto, "If it's man-made, it can be moved, with enough men, equipment, and money!"

Mr. Willis J. Watson had a son, Tex Jackson Watson, who helped his father from his early childhood until he took over the business when his father became disabled and died in the late eighties.

A Call from God

In the fall of 1988, I was busy putting the finishing touches of a Case dozer, so that I could deliver it to McDonough, Georgia. Our tractor business located on Highway 247 Connector and Interstate I-75 had been a busy place that week as we rushed to complete two tractors and the dozer before we closed on Saturday afternoon.

After double-checking the dozer, I loaded it on a new gooseneck trailer that was connected to my faithful Chevrolet dually truck. We used four heavy chains to securely tie the dozer to the trailer. I glanced at my watch, it was almost 3:00 p.m. and I knew if I could leave now, I could deliver the dozer to McDonough and return in time to help lock up the business for the weekend. The gooseneck trailer was brand new, so I checked the lights and brakes before I left to be sure they were working properly.

Then I walked back to my office to pick up the paperwork and I saw my cousin Tex Watson park right in front of the office. I was glad to see Tex and I asked him if he could go with me on the delivery, so we could get a chance to talk. We had always helped each other when needed and I figured we could discuss how his business was and I could fill him in on my business activities.

Tex quickly accepted my offer and in only a couple of minutes from the time he arrived, we were in my Chevy truck driving out the gate toward the highway when I heard the telephone ringer on the outside of the building. For some reason I stopped, normally I would have pressed the

140

accelerator to the floor and just let my brother and business partner take care of the call. I just had a strange feeling the call was important. I shifted the transmission into reverse and I backed the trailer back inside the gate.

Suddenly, my brother, Rudy, yelled, "It's for Tex. Wanda said to come right home. It's important."

I was very disappointed and Tex said, "Well, maybe we can go next time."

Then I drove out the gate and headed toward Interstate I-75 and proceeded north. When I approached the Hartley Bridge Road exit, I had to slow down, because of road construction, and because of an accident that was being investigated by a Bibb County Sheriff's Deputy. The accident was only a fender-bender, so I cruised on by at about forty-five miles per hour with the other traffic.

Then suddenly, one of the construction workers in the median raised his hand to stop traffic in the left hand lane to let a big dump truck out. I let off the accelerator, but I was right in the right hand land and another worker was waving for us to continue on. Suddenly a little white hatchback in the left lane turned in front of me. He was apparently stopping for the worker's signal when he decided to change into my lane instead. I slammed on the brakes, but I couldn't stop my 20,000 pound rig in twenty feet and I gently bumped the little hatchback.

The number one most noticeable part of the car was two small children sitting in their child safety seats in the back of the little compact. The instant I bumped the car,

141

the car bounced about thirty feet and then the irate driver slammed on brakes.

Until now the damage to my truck was zero and the damage to the little car would be minor. So now he stops dead still ahead of me. I'm still on my brakes, but they won't stop my truck and trailer before striking the car again.

My brain is racing as I realize that I can't stop that quickly! I can't pass on the right, because of some temporary concrete barriers, so I glance left and hope I can get in front of the big dump truck pulling onto the left lane from the median. I instantly steer left hoping I can miss the little car now sitting perfectly still with its red brake lights shining!

I would have made it, except for the right rear tire on my dual rear wheel truck. As I braced for another impact, all I could think about were those two precious little children in the rear seat of that car. I just couldn't believe the driver had slammed on the brakes after being bumped by my truck after he suddenly changed lanes.

If he had just let the car roll about fifty yards to the exit ramp, I could have stopped my truck and then followed him up the exit ramp to wait for the Sheriff's car we had just passed to write up an accident report for us.

My right rear tire caught the left rear bumper of the little car and spun it around like a top causing my one ton truck to swerve to the right and the trailer jack-knifed to the right.

The accident seemed to happen in slow motion, as the little car slammed into the guardrail and overturned. Then all four chains on the trailer broke under the sudden impact and the dozer started sliding off the flatbed trailer and wound up on top of the upside down car that was wedged between my Chevrolet truck and the gooseneck trailer as the heavy steel gooseneck plate bolted in the bed of my truck ripped loose and the whole mess slid sideways for about one hundred feet.

As the dust settled, I reached to unlock my shoulder seatbelt and suddenly realized that the left portion of the dozer's blade had penetrated the cab of my truck and had stopped only inches from me.

I didn't have time to dwell on the fact that a dozer blade was in the front seat with me, because all I could think about were those two little children who are now hanging upside down in their safety seats in a little compact car that is under a dozer and wedged between my truck and a twenty-five foot dual wheel tandem trailer.

I had the seatbelt unfastened and the driver's door open in less than a second, as I raced around the truck to save the kids. A dump truck driver had stopped and he and I got to the window of the little car at the same time.

The driver unbuckled himself and was trying to get out of the car.

The truck driver and I yelled, "Hand us the kids," but he just looked at us, as if he was in shock.

The truck driver broke the driver's side rear view mirror off of the car and climbed into what was left of the car and unbuckled the screaming children and handed them to me.

I was never more relieved in my life that both children were alright. A young woman suddenly appeared beside me and she took the children and carried them to safety on the other side of the concrete barrier.

A Macon-Bibb County emergency rescue team arrived within minutes and they checked the kids and the other driver and found them to be fine. A fire truck pulled up beside the tangled mess ready to extinguish a fire, if the car's gas tank erupted when the dozer was driven across the bottom of the little car and back on the bed of the trailer and then to make a sharp turn and go down the ramps to reach the pavement.

Unfortunately, I had to drive the dozer and it was sitting on the car's gas tank. The fire truck was used to stabilize the gooseneck trailer that had been completely ripped free from my truck. The fireman had a big water hose ready, just in case the steel tracks of the dozer ripped the gas tank open and started a fire.

As I cautiously climbed up onto the dozer, I realized that when the accident occurred, it happened so fast that I didn't have time to get scared. I was too busy trying to evade the little hatchback with the two kids, but now I had a stomach full of butterflies, as I surveyed the dangerous job at hand.

One of the rescue workers said, "Don't worry if it catches fire, we can put it out!"

I yelled, "What if it explodes?"

The rescue guy yelled, "It will be your wife's lucky day!"

A WMAZ television crew had entered the scene and I figured, if the tank exploded, I'll make the evening news as a crispy critter.

I looked up at the sky and said, "Thank you for saving the kids and if you don't mind, I could use a little help here."

Then I started the dozer's diesel engine and tried to back the blade out of my pickup's cab, but the entire truck came with it. I stopped and grabbed the left turn handle on the dozer and I grabbed the dozer blade's tilt angle lever with my right hand. I glanced around at the hundred or so people watching my every move, not to mention the television camera, and as I hit the throttle, the dozer's blade pulled free from the cab of my truck and I found myself balancing myself on top of an overturned car as I slowly backed the dozer onto the bed of the trailer.

I turned the dozer hard left as I drove the dozer backwards down the ramps and parked it on the pavement. I heard a real loud cheer and applause as I shut the engine off and hopped down from the big yellow tractor.

I walked over to examine what was left of my one ton Chevy dually and I was amazed at the damage. The right rear fiberglass fender was shattered and the tire and wheel were damaged, the front end was smashed by the guard rail, the gooseneck mounting plate had been ripped out of the rear bed, but the hole in the passenger's side door was gigantic. The dozer blade had penetrated the cab almost to the middle of the front seat.

Then suddenly, it occurred to me, what if Wanda had not called my business and asked for Tex to come home. He would have been killed by the dozer blade. I wondered how she knew Tex was at my business. He had been driving by and saw me getting into my truck and stopped to ask me something. He had only been at my business about two minutes when Wanda had made the call.

Ackerman's Wrecker Service did a professional job and transported the truck, trailer, and dozer back to my business and I called Tex to tell him what had happened.

Tex said, "When I got home I asked Wanda how she knew where I was and why she had called?"

Wanda said, "I don't know. I was walking down the hall with some laundry in my hands and I felt a chill come over me and I ran to the phone and called your shop to get Tex to come home."

We were all amazed at what had happened! We knew that the Almighty had saved Tex's life and we were all very grateful.

Three Hundred Dollar Bills

It was an unusually warm December day as I worked in my farm tractor business in Byron, Georgia, just off I-75. A man named Doc came by to pay me for a 4000 Ford diesel tractor and some equipment. We had negotiated and settled on a sales price of $6300.00. I wrote up the Bill of Sale and Doc signed it as the Buyer, then he pulled a small brown paper sack out of his coat pocket and opened the bag and removed a stack of one hundred dollar bills as he said, "I've been saving up to buy me a tractor for several years and I can't wait to put it to work."

As he talked he stacked the money on my desk and then he said, "Go ahead and count it!"

I was a little reluctant, because I'm a clumsy money counter and in over twenty-five years of being in this business, every time I counted the money, it was right. So I said, "I'm sure it's right."

But no, he insisted I count the money, so I did. I counted sixty, one hundred dollar bills.

The man said, "No, you miscounted, do it again."

So I counted out loud again and only come up with sixty.

So Doc grabbed the cash and said, "I know I had $6000.00 in this bag and I put three more one hundred dollar bills in this sack before I left home. So Doc counted the bills and came up with just sixty.

He looked a little shocked as he said, "I'm going to count it again."

This time he counted very slowly, one, two, three, four and on until he finished the pile of bills at sixty.

Now, if you passed second grade math, then you would know that sixty, one hundred dollar bills would only total six thousand dollars, not the six thousand, three hundred we agreed on.

Doc looked a little bewildered as he said, "I would have bet my life I had sixty-three, one hundred dollar bills in this bag."

Then he smiled and said, "My son is with me and he is taking accounting in college. He walked to the door and yelled for his son to come in.

As his son entered, his father introduced us and we shook hands, then his father handed his son the stack of money and said, "Son, please count this cash for us old, feeble-minded people.

So the son took the cash and counted up six thousand dollars.

His father said, "Son, count that again. There's supposed to be $6300.00 in that stack."

So his son counted again and come up with only six thousand dollars.

I felt sorry for Doc; because I was sure he thought there was sixty-three, hundred dollar bills in the small bag. I said, "Look, it's alright. You can give me the other three, hundred dollar bills later." I went ahead and wrote "Paid in Full" by cash on the sales ticket and handed Doc his copy.

Poor Doc looked so frustrated. I really felt sorry for him, but I knew he was a good man, so I showed my faith in him by writing "Paid in Full" on the ticket and just started explaining to him and his son some of the features on the tractor.

As I talked, I could tell Doc wasn't focused on the tractor. It was only Tuesday and I wasn't supposed to deliver the tractor and equipment until Saturday afternoon, so I said, "I'll show you how to operate everything when I deliver it on Saturday afternoon."

Doc and his son were about to leave when Doc turned around and said, "My wife is coming down here to shop at the mall across the interstate tomorrow and I'll have her bring you three hundred more dollars."

I said, "Sure that will be fine."

Doc looked relieved as he reached out to shake my hand and said, "I wasn't trying to cheat you."

I said, "I know you weren't. You insisted that I count the money. If you were trying to cheat me, you wouldn't have done that."

So the man and his son drove away and I put the sack of money in my coat pocket and went back to work.

149

The next morning my wife come by the shop and asked me, if I needed her to do anything and I thought about the cash in my coat pocket, so I told her to make out a deposit ticket for $6300.00.

I always kept $500.00 to $1000.00 in cash in case some emergency came up after banking hours, so I put three, one hundred dollar bills in the bag to make the deposit and the bank match our book work and the sales ticket.

There was absolutely no doubt in my mind that Doc's wife would be coming by with the other $300.00 and I could put it back in my emergency fund envelope.

So my wife went to the bank and I went back to work.

I had told my wife about the money situation the night before and she said I did the right thing to trust Doc.

My wife got to the bank and handed the sack full of money to the teller and the deposit ticket for $6300.00.

The teller ran the pile of cash through one of those fancy high speed counters and then she said, "What should I do with the extra three hundred dollars?"

My wife was so shocked, she just stood there staring at the teller thinking about the story that I had told her the night before.

The teller said, "Do you want to change the deposit to $6600.00 or do you want the three hundred dollars back?"

My wife had the teller run the money through the machine again and it came up $6600.00. She told the teller the story about the three hundred dollars.

The teller said, "See, this proves it. Men should let women handle the money!"

So my wife walked out of the bank with a $6300.00 deposit receipt and three, one hundred dollar bills. Then she called me and told me about the extra money.

I couldn't believe it. Doc, his son, and I counted the money twice. How could this happen. I remembered that Doc's wife was going to bring us three hundred dollars, so I looked up Doc's phone number and called him with the good news.

Doc was very excited and I heard him yell, "I was right son, there was sixty-three hundred dollars in that sack."

I was relieved.

Doc laughed and said, "I knew it. I knew it. I knew it!"

After the excitement was over, I reminded Doc that I had already written "Paid in Full" on his Bill of Sale and that he didn't have to send his wife by my shop with the money.

Doc said, "Well, she's already left and should be there any minute."

I said, "I'll just tell her what happened and send her on her way."

Doc yelled, "No, no, no, no. You keep the money. Don't tell her. Don't tell her!"

I couldn't believe my ears. Now, why in the world would he want me to keep the money?

Doc said, "Just take the money and don't tell her anything."

I was confused. Why would he want me to take money that he didn't owe me!

Then Doc continued, "She's on her way to do some Christmas shopping. She would spend every dime. Take the money and I'll come by next week and pick it up."

I remember standing there holding the telephone to my ear and thinking: This can't be real. I must be dreaming.

As I was trying to figure out, if this is really happening or was I having a dream or maybe a nightmare, Doc says, "My wife is normally very careful with our money, but she loves Christmas so much that last year she even bought Boris a present."

I said, "Boris."

Doc explained, "Boris is the neighbor's dog."

After I finally realized I wasn't asleep, I agreed to just hold the money for Doc and not tell his wife.

As I placed the phone back on the receiver, the door opened and in walked a lady with an envelope in her hand.

She says, "I'm Doc's wife and he told me to bring you three hundred dollars and she handed me the envelope."

I could tell by the look in her eyes that she wasn't happy.

Then she said, "I want a receipt for the money."

I explained that I had already written "Paid in Full" on her husband's Bill of Sale, but she still wanted a receipt. I wanted to tell her what had happened, but then Doc wouldn't be happy, so I wrote her a receipt and she put it in her purse and said, "Merry Christmas."

Then she turned and walked out the door.

I felt bad. I wanted to tell her, but I had told her husband I wouldn't.

In a few days Doc came by and I gave him the three hundred dollars and told him I would appreciate it, if he would tell his wife.

He just laughed and said, "Ok, I'll tell her after Christmas shopping is over." Doc just shook my hand and left.

As he drove away, I thought, "How could three hundred dollars cause so much confusion."

SHERLOCK

In days gone by, when I was a building contractor, I became good friends with a man named Tommy. Tommy smoked a pipe, had a flat top haircut and was one of the smartest and nicest men I ever met. Tommy ran a large hardware store that I shopped at on an almost daily basis. I came to respect this man's judgment and character and sought his advice on many occasions. My father lived over sixty miles away, so I adopted him as a source of wisdom and encouragement, when I needed it.

Now Tommy was a big coon hunter and he was always telling me about his weekend hunting trips and about his hunting dogs. Tommy had more pictures of his hunting dogs than his family on the wall behind his desk. Now don't get me wrong, Tommy loved his family and was a solid citizen, but his favorite subject was hunting. For years Tommy would tell me about his latest hunt. Once he got started, you best grab a chair and relax, because you weren't going anywhere till the hunt was over.

One spring day when I entered the hardware store, Tommy called me to his side to show me a picture. It was a picture of a hunting dog. As he showed me the picture, he explained that this was no ordinary hunting dog, but it was of a special breed from a special family that raises the best hunting dogs in America. He went on to explain that this dog was a certified, professionally trained dog like no other on earth.

From the gleam in his eyes, you would have thought he was showing you a picture of his first grandchild. I looked at the dog in the picture and tried to look impressed, but all I saw was a hound dog. For the next few weeks, every time I entered the store, he gave me an update on this wonderfully trained, very special hunting dog.

One day I asked him why he didn't just go buy the dog, if it's so special to him. That's when he told me the price. The owner wanted $5000.00 cash for the dog and he would have to go to Texas to get it. Now at that time $5000.00 would buy you a new compact car or a make a nice down payment on a house. Day after day, when I entered his store, I would see Tommy admiring a picture of that dog. I had a feeling he wanted that dog more than anything on earth, but he wanted somebody to give him the encouragement to go to Texas and buy it. Tommy was a successful business man, and he could afford to pay the $5000.00, if he wanted the dog bad enough, so I asked him, "Do you want this dog?"

Tommy just stood there looking at the picture grinning like a timber wolf with its fresh kill.

I continued, "Tommy you don't drink, take drugs, beat your wife and kids or gamble, do you?"

Tommy looked a little shocked by my question as he shook his head and said, "No, of course not!"

I said, "Then, if you want this dog so bad, call the man right now and tell him you are coming after this prized animal!"

155

To my surprise he grabbed me and shook me and said, "You're right, I'm going to call right now!" As Tommy raced to the phone I used this opportunity to escape and went to work.

The next night I came home late. I had worked till after dark. I took a shower and had just sat down to a nice meal, when I heard a horn blowing in the driveway. It was Tommy in his red and white Chevrolet Silverado pickup, and he was backing up our driveway. Tommy had a fancy cage built on the back of his pick up for transporting hunting dogs. The cage had a cover to protect the dogs from rain and of course a thick carpet for them to lie on. Most humans on earth didn't get treated as well as one of Tommy's dogs.

Tommy was so excited; he couldn't wait to show me his new hunting dog. The smile on his face showed he was the happiest man on earth, and I was happy for him. He ran up to me and gave me a big bear hug and said, "I want to thank you for giving me the encouragement to buy this wonderful dog."

I said, "Well, you're welcome Tommy, and I'm sure the two of you will become an excellent team."

As we stood behind the truck, the dog raced around in the cage and barked while Tommy pointed out what perfect breeding this dog had. I learned more about hunting dogs in the next half hour than I really wanted to know, but as my meal waited on the dining table, I listened to this very happy man go on and on about this new dog. I was so hungry that my stomach was growling as loud as the dog was barking. Tommy was explaining how the dog's colors made it exceptional and then how rare this breed was and, of course, how smart it was. When I was beginning to think I would starve before he concluded the detailed explanation of the dog's fine qualities, Tommy looked at his watch and said, "It's almost 10 o'clock, I better get home and show it to my wife before she goes to bed."

Tommy thanked me again for encouraging him to buy the dog of all dogs, and left as suddenly as he arrived. I couldn't believe it, he had drove to Texas and back to get this dog and showed it to me before he went home. Well I don't really care that much for dogs but if Tommy was happy that was good with me.

Finally, I got to eat and I joined my wife in the family room to watch a late movie when the phone rang. It was Tommy. Apparently he had forgotten some of the dog's fine points and he continued to rave about the dog.

On Monday morning I went to Tommy's hardware store for some supplies. Tommy saw me coming and grabbed my hand and led me to the sales counter where he had about a dozen large color photographs of this dog on the wall. I wondered how he got those big color pictures made over the weekend. Tommy was happier than a five year old playing in a mud puddle. He was trying to decide on a name for the dog.

I asked him, "What is the best characteristic of the dog?"

Tommy dropped into a deep train of thought and then he yelled, "He's the smartest dog on earth!"

A woman standing nearby volunteered, "How about Einstein?"

Tommy shook his head and said, "No, that's not a good dog name!"

Another man in the crowd suggested, "Sherlock Holmes."

Tommy looked up and said, "That's not bad, but too long."

I said, "What about Sherlock?"

Tommy yelled, "That's it, Sherlock, that's perfect!"

Tommy raced to the telephone and called someone and said, "Sherlock, that's what I want engraved on my new dog's collar." Then he asked, "Do you have any gold dog tags?" Then he smirked and said, "Brass will be alright."

While Tommy ordered his dog's collar and tag, I paid the cashier and went to work.

For the next few weeks when I entered his store, Tommy would fill me in on his dog's latest achievements. He explained that he was working with Sherlock to develop a bond between them before they went on their first hunt together. I just patiently listened and tried to act like I was excited just like Tommy.

One day when I entered the store, Tommy ran to me and said, "The 18th, that's this Friday, will be our first hunt together, and I can't wait!"

That weekend I took my wife and daughter to the beach. When we returned on Monday, I went by Tommy's store to pickup a few things and I was ready for a good report on Sherlock. When I arrived at the sales counter, I saw his partner Mr. Bradshaw and I asked, "Where's Tommy?"

Mr. Bradshaw was busy looking at some papers, but he laid them down and looked at me with a somber look and said, "We're not sure!"

I was shocked. Tommy was always at the store during the week. I asked, "What's wrong?"

Mr. Bradshaw walked over to the sales counter. Mr. Bradshaw looked very worried as he said, "Tommy turned that new dog of his loose Friday night and when the hunt was over it didn't come back!"

I just stood there looking at Mr. Bradshaw, how could this be possible with such an expensive, supposedly well trained dog I wondered? Then it occurred to me that I was the moron that talked him into buying that very special dog. I had a sick feeling deep down in my stomach, as I remembered what he said that night in my driveway. Tommy thanked me for encouraging him to buy that dog.

Then, with a long face, Mr. Bradshaw said, "Tommy hasn't been home since. He told the other hunters he wasn't coming home until he found that dog!"

Then it occurred to me, this could be a joke and Tommy was probably in his office waiting to step out and say "surprise!" I walked around the end of the sales counter and looked in Tommy's office, but he wasn't there. I looked back at Mr. Bradshaw and said, "Please tell me this didn't really happen, that it's a joke or something."

Mr. Bradshaw just slowly shook his head and said, "I've never been more serious in my life!"

For one of the very few times in my life, I was speechless. The somber mood of everybody in the store was overpowering. I walked out slowly. All I could think about was I gave him the encouragement to buy that dog. I felt lower than a rat in a gopher hole. Why did I have to be the one that caused this to happen? I felt terrible. If only I had kept my big mouth shut, Tommy probably wouldn't have bought that dog.

Several days went by and I didn't go to his store. I felt so sorry for Tommy. When a coon hunter loses a dog like this, especially such an expensive and special dog, it's almost like losing a loved one. I just didn't know what to say or do. A couple of weeks went by and I saw Tommy's red and white Silverado pickup parked out front of the hardware store. I knew that sooner or later I had to face my old friend again. I had always admired and respected Tommy and I knew this wasn't going to be easy.

My mind once again wondered back to my driveway that night, when he thanked me for giving him encouragement to buy that dog. I entered the store trying to remember, if my life insurance was paid up, and walked to the front counter. I saw Mr. Bradshaw and I asked, "Where's Tommy?"

Mr. Bradshaw looked up from his computer screen and whispers, "He's in his office. He just sits there and looks at the pictures on the wall."

I just stood there for a moment, then I said, "I guess I'll just come back later."

Mr. Bradshaw looked distressed as he said, "No, you're the one that talked him into buying that dog and you're the one that needs to talk to him."

I swallowed really hard, but the lump in my throat was as big as a brick. I walked to the door that led to Tommy's office and took one more breath and turned the door knob. Tommy turned to face me as I said, "I know what happened to that darned dog!"

Tommy's face turned from sad to shock.

As I continued, "I wasn't going to tell you, but a friend of mine saw a pretty blond haired young lady driving a black Corvette convertible with Texas plates pick that dog up near Junction Corner the next morning after he disappeared and they sped away going west on Highway 80."

Tommy's face showed even more shock as he said, "Red!" I just stared at him as he stood up and said, "Red!"

I wondered what he was saying!

Then he said, "If this story is going to cost me $5000.00, I want that darned Corvette to be red!"

Now, I was shocked as we just stood there staring at each other. Suddenly, I saw the corners of his mouth start to turn, and then I saw his eyes blink as a big smile took over his face.

Then I yelled, "Alright, it was a red Corvette!"

Tommy started laughing, I started laughing. Mr. Bradshaw and everybody in the store started laughing. Tommy walked over to me and gave me a big bear hug and said, "I always liked red corvettes!"

Everybody in the store laughed, as I turned and walked out of the store. I was so relieved to see a smile on Tommy's face. I decided right then and there, if I ever hear someone else talking about buying a $5000.00 hunting dog, I'm going to put one foot in my mouth and hop away on the other one!

Flash Back

On a recent trip to South Georgia, my cell phone rang as I entered the city limits of Helena. The caller was a fellow Farm Show Magazine subscriber and he wanted some information about a recent article about running diesel engines on gasoline.

As I crossed the railroad tracks, I turned left and drove around the City Square and parked beside the Seaboard Railroad. As I completed the call and was about to drive away, my memory bank flashed back to when I was four years old and lived on a farm just four miles north of this very special little town.

On that fateful warm fall Friday morning, I was playing in our back yard, when suddenly I heard a giant KA-BOOM! I was absolutely terrified! I had never heard anything so horrible in my life!

Within seconds my Mom ran out the back door and picked me up and then ran back toward our house.

My Dad suddenly appeared at the back door with a completely shocked look on his face and yelled, "What in the world was that?"

My Mom was holding me so tight I could hardly breathe as she replied, "I don't know!"

Then Dad pointed toward the south and yelled, "Look!" As a big ball of smoke was rising in the sky, my Dad then yelled, "It must be a bomb, we might be in another war!"

163

My Mom asked, "Why would anyone bomb Helena?"

My Dad reached over and took me from my Mother's arms and exclaimed, "It's the crossroads of four major US highways, two railroads, and it has the biggest turpentine plant in the world!"

My Mom asked, "Why would anyone want to bomb a turpentine plant?"

Then Dad replied, "Turpentine is used to make explosives!"

Before I knew what was going on, we were in our Ford car traveling over 80 miles per hour while Mom and Dad discussed the possible reasons for the big KA-BOOM!

As we raced toward Helena, we saw many cars parked along the side of the road and Dad remarked that almost all of them had out- of- state tags. Apparently, the road we lived on was used by lots of people from up north to reach Jacksonville and Daytona Beach, Florida. Dad said the KA-BOOM must have scared the tourist, so they stopped and were trying to figure out what had happened.

As Dad passed slower cars, he turned our car's radio on and tuned it to the local station.

The radio announcer said, "And to repeat this bulletin, a propane gas tank has exploded in the City of Helena and at least one person is dead and dozens are injured, some critically." The announcer continued, "City officials are pleading for help to rescue survivors from the rubble and to give blood at the Telfair Medical Clinic."

Apparently several large buildings had been destroyed in the explosion and bricks, glass, wood, and metal roofing had rained down on pedestrians and motorists alike along the main street.

The announcer is quiet for a few seconds as he receives more information. Then he says, "The Helena fire truck was destroyed in the blast and fire trucks from McRae and surrounding towns were in route."

As we reached the city limits, all we could see was fire, smoke, and dust reaching miles into the sky and blocking out the sunlight. It was like night time at 10:00 a.m.

Dad drove around several cars that had been abandoned in the street, then turned left at the City Square, made a U-turn and parked beside the Seaboard Railroad. Dad opened his door and told us to stay in the car and to blow the car's horn, if we needed him.

Then, my Dad ran across the street and helped some men lift a sign and a section of roofing to help free a man and woman trapped by the debris.

We saw an old pickup truck cross the road in front of us. It was driven by Mrs. Fate Wilson. The Wilsons lived in a little wooden house just down the hill from where the propane tank had been. Mrs. Wilson had been watering her flowers when the explosion occurred and she was blown nearly one hundred feet and landed in a ditch. She had first crawled and then walked to check on her husband working in his small workshop in their backyard, but the entire shop was gone. She walked around in the dust and smoke until

165

she found a big pile of boards and roofing tin. She started calling her husband's name as she removed board after board from the pile.

When she heard him moaning, she worked even harder until she pulled him from the debris and then carried him over her shoulder to her husband's old pickup truck. She then drove him to the Telfair Medical Clinic. She had never driven a car before, but she had saved her husband's life.

Mr. Wilson had to have nearly fifty stitches before the bleeding stopped. He had been sewed up by the town's veterinarian who was visiting a friend at the hospital when the blast occurred. The veterinarian had been a paramedic during World War II and had gone to veterinary school afterwards on the G.I. Bill.

Two boys who had been riding their bikes in front of the post office were so severely injured by the falling debris that they had to be rushed to the Macon hospital's trauma center. Dr. Born, a local physician, rode in the ambulance to Macon with the two boys in an effort to keep them alive. They apparently had internal injuries and both survived.

A waitress from a nearby hotel found a little girl wearing a white dress that was splattered with blood wandering aimlessly around, unattended. The waitress asked the little girl where her parents were and she led her to her mother who was trapped in the rubble under a store awning. Amazingly, the little girl was unharmed, but her mother had been seriously injured, but survived the ordeal.

Thousands of bricks that had been blown off of the stores next to the propane tank and were piled up to three feet deep in the street. Police, firemen, as well as volunteers worked tirelessly to be sure no one else was trapped in the debris.

When the radio station asked for people to give blood, so many people showed up at the Telfair Medical Clinic that many had to be turned away.

Many people said it was a miracle that only one person, the propane gas truck operator, had been killed, but many people carried the scars and injuries from this tragedy for the rest of their lives.

Twenty-four hours later the streets had been cleared and workmen started rebuilding the damaged stores and shops along Main Street. Workers actually cleaned and used most of the bricks recovered from the streets to rebuild the walls of the buildings. Much like the crack in the Liberty Bell, you can still see a sort of zig-zag line that starts near ground level at the rear of the stores and works its way upward toward the roof line on the front. It's like a historical marker of sort that recorded the events of a warm fall day in 1954 in the special little town of Helena.

This story should remind us that in any moment a totally unexpected tragedy can suddenly change our lives forever! You know it seems like in our darkest hours is when God's brightest light shines on us! With his love and mercy we can help each other to handle the tragedies in life!

Strange Encounter

It was a typical fall morning as I exited my home for my short drive to our tractor business until I saw something strange on my doorsteps. I stopped to pick up a somewhat tattered envelope, and I wondered who had left it on our porch. It was simply addressed to "Resident Defendant."

As I opened the letter and began to read the poorly written correspondence, I realized I was being threatened with legal action by a family of squirrels who apparently live on our small farm. I must admit I was completely shocked as I continued to read. The squirrels were complaining that I had been greedily hoarding the pecans from our five acre grove that surrounds our home. The letter said that by the laws of nature they were declaring their legal rights to half of our crop and that my failure to comply with the squirrel's demands could land me in court. The letter was signed by F. Lee Chipmunk, Attorney at Law.

I was flabbergasted. I immediately reached for my trusty cell phone and called Max B. Asbell, a retired lawyer and good friend, and I asked him if he had ever had any litigation involving squirrels.

After a short silence, he responded, "No, I can't remember any litigation involving squirrels, but I definitely encountered my share of nuts."

Then I read the letter to Mr. Asbell over the phone.

He responded, "I don't think I have ever heard of a court that controls the laws of nature and if there is one, I don't think you would be legally bound by it."

As Mr.Asbell spoke, I listened closely. Then he said, "Since man is at the top of the pecking order in nature, you would only be held accountable by a city, county, state, or federal court, and of course, by your wife."

I thanked Mr. Asbell for his opinion and then I heard a terrible screeching sound. It was an alarm clock! Apparently my encounter with a squirrel's legal threat was just a nightmare.

As I crawled out of bed, while trying to get both eyes to open at the same time, I didn't say a thing to my wife about the nightmare. After my wake up shower and morning shave, I scoffed down my breakfast, got dressed, and hugged my wife and walked toward the back door. As I grabbed the door knob, I just froze perfectly still for a few seconds. Then I asked my wife, "Would you please look out the back door and see if everything is alright?"

My wife opened the back door and said, "Everything looks alright to me."

I asked, "Are you sure? Do you see any squirrels?" I said, "Last night I had a nightmare."

My wife said, "Never mind. I've heard enough of your crazy dreams to last me a lifetime."

I peeped outside as my wife said, "Besides I could easily understand why one of the biggest nuts would be concerned about squirrels!"

As I cautiously walked toward my trusty Ford F-150, I realized how lucky I am to have a wonderful wife and kids and a friend like Max B. Asbell.

I hope you enjoyed reading my stories as much as I enjoyed writing them. I hope that you will tell your friends and relatives about *Brown's Pine Ridge Stories.* I will write short stories and I will publish novels under the *Brown's Pine Ridge Stories* series.

A high school teacher tried to get me to become a writer, but I couldn't believe that anybody would read my stories.

After graduating from high school and working my way through college, I became a building contractor. I soon learned I enjoyed buying old run-down houses and restoring them to like-new condition. Then, when the housing industry collapsed in the early 1980's, my younger brother and I started a tractor and equipment business. We bought old, ugly used tractors and reconditioned them like-new. I finally realized I had the ability to see a beautiful pearl inside that plain old oyster.

I now realize it was my high school teacher, Miss Barbara Ann Davidson, who saw something special in me and tried to convince me to become a writer. I promised her before she died that I would make a serious effort to become a writer. I would be forever humbled, if you would help me to fulfill her dream for my life.

I dedicate this book to the late Barbara Ann Rowland!

I would like to hear from you. My email address is gcbrown2011@windstream.net. My mailing address is Gary C. Brown, 2831 US Hwy 41 N, Fort Valley, GA

31030.   My phone number is 478-954-1283 or 478-956-3169.

You can also order Brown's Pine Ridge Stories at amazon.com.

Thank you.

Gary C. Brown

Made in the USA
Columbia, SC
26 April 2017